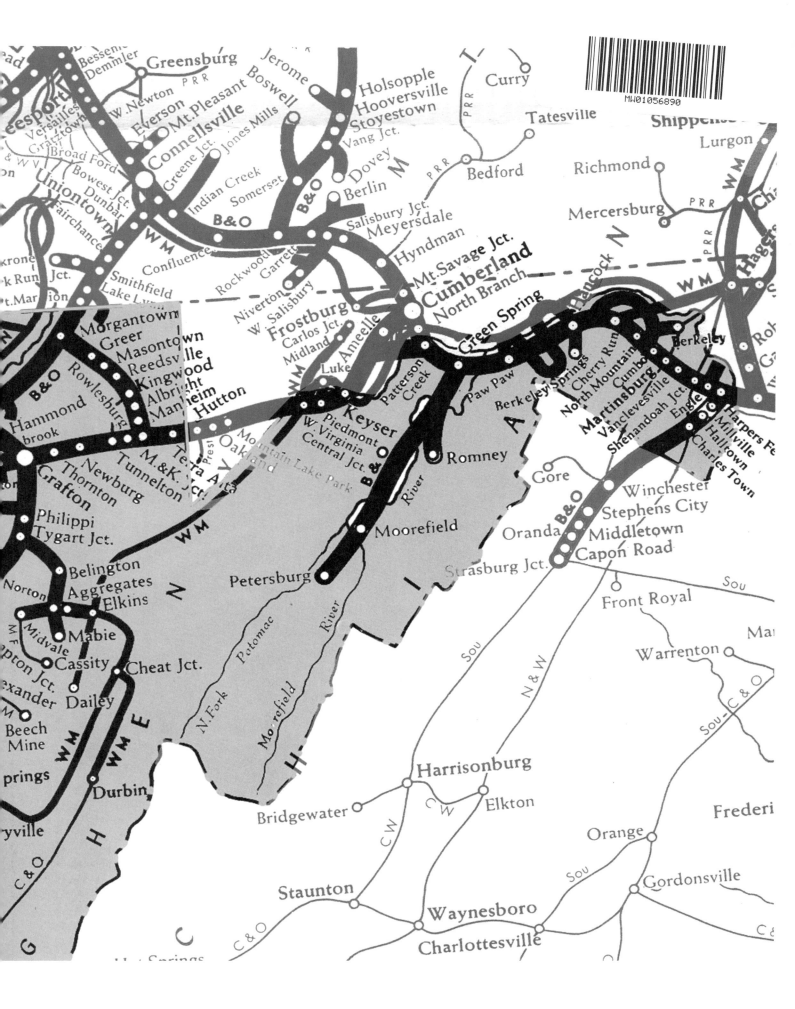

TLC Publishing Inc.
18292 Forest Rd.
Forest, Virginia 24551
434-385-4076
www.tlcrailroadbooks.com

© Copyright 2011 TLC Publishing, Inc.
All Rights Reserved
No part of this book may be reproduced without
written permission of the publisher, except for
brief excerpts used in reviews, etc.

ISBN 9780939487509

Digital Photo Production, Design, and Layout
by
Karen Parker

Printed in the U.S.A. by
Walsworth Printing Company, Marceline, Mo.

Front Cover: The engineer aboard Class EM-1 2-8-8-4 No. 7622 has his locomotive exerting all 115,000 pounds of tractive effort as it and two articulated pushers which are out of sight advance an eastbound Timesaver over the steepest part of Cranberry Grade west of Terra Alta ca. 1947. (Bruce D. Fales photo, Jay Williams Collection, colorized by Karen Parker)

Title Page: Two 2-8-8-0 helpers, Class EL-5a 7153 and Class EL-3a 7133, do all they can to assist a heavy coal train, making only about 5 miles an hour. (R.H. Kindig photo, TLC Collection)

Facing Page: Flagman A.C. Westfall, with train orders in his coat pocket, stands by the open trap of coach 3692 on Train 11 at Clarksburg on April 8, 1966. He seems to be beckoning to readers to climb aboard and tour B&O's West Virginia lines via the pages of this book. (Photo by Bob Withers)

Back Cover Top Left: Flagman Charlie Morrow responds to his engineer's four long toots and returns to the warmth of coach 3565 on Train 12, the eastbound Metropolitan, which had been waiting at Berkeley Run Junction, just west of Grafton, for counterpart Train 11, now whipping up the snow at left. It's 3:40 p.m. on Sunday, Jan. 23, 1966, and bone-chilling cold. A railfan photographer/passenger on No. 12 is afraid he'll be left behind. (Photo by Bob Withers)

Back Cover Top Right: Baltimore & Ohio's famous Salt Lick curve near Terra Alta, W. Va. is the locale of this early 1960s photo showing a mixture of model F-7 cab-unit diesels and road switchers eastbound with a heavy coal train. Steep grades for eastbound coal were a challenge for the B&O, as they were for all of West Virginia's major railroads. (TLC Collection)

Back Cover Center Left: Operator Claire Gibbs prepares to hand up orders to Train 12, the eastbound Metropolitan Special, at SX Tower in Parkersburg's Low Yard, at 2:11 p.m. on Friday, July 5, 1963. The National Limited and Metropolitan Special are being detoured via New Martinsville because of the a tunnel project between Parkersburg and Clarksburg, on the Baltimore–St. Louis main line, which crosses overhead in the background. (Photo by Bob Withers)

Back Cover Center Right: It's 7:04 p.m. on Friday, July 5, 1963, and second-trick operator Betty Martin Lehew has relieved Claire Gibbs at SX Tower. She is all business at the moment, repeating a train order to the dispatcher that she will deliver to departing Huntington-bound freight No. 93 a little later. Technically, tonight's train is a "mixed"; Friday is one of three weeknights on which the train's crews must permit paying passengers to ride in the caboose behind the locomotive. (Photo by Bob Withers)

Back Cover Bottom: Train 23 is ready to depart Parkersburg's Sixth Street Station for Cincinnati at 11 a.m. on Wednesday, July 3, 1963. Other trains are being detoured between Clarksburg and Parkersburg during the months-long tunnel enlargement/elimination project mentioned above, but No. 23's through passengers have been bused across the gap. (Photo by Bob Withers)

Table of Contents

Foreword

This is the third volume in our series of books on the railroads of West Virginia. The first volume gave an overview of all the major railroads operating in the state, Volume 2 was about the Chesapeake & Ohio Railway, while the present volume is about the Baltimore & Ohio Railroad.

The B&O was the first railroad to build into what is now West Virginia, at that time still a part of Virginia. Before the War Between the States and the separation of West Virginia from Virginia in 1863, B&O had built two major main lines across the northern part of the state, the first reaching Wheeling, and the second farther south to Parkersburg, where a crossing of the Ohio River allowed connection with other railroads. By 1857 B&O had a through service between the coast at Baltimore and St. Louis via Parkersburg. The connecting lines were later incorporated into the B&O system, as were other lines connecting at Wheeling, and through Pennsylvania at Pittsburgh, and on to Chicago.

By 1900 the B&O system was largely complete, with only the coal territories to experience further development and expansion in the two decades ahead. In West Virginia the opening of coal lands made coal the main commodity B&O hauled. In the years to come,

West Virginia supplied a large portion of B&O's coal business, with the production going both east and west.

B&O's through passenger business across the state was concentrated on the Parkersburg line, as it became a main Washington-Cincinnati-St. Louis artery.

Other lines included a connection through the center of the state to the capital at Charleston, and a line down the Ohio River from Wheeling through Parkersburg and Huntington to Kenova.

Author Bob Withers, well known for his several B&O-subject books, has prepared a general overview of B&O operations and facilities in West Virginia, complemented by a large and diverse selection of photos from the late steam and early diesel era. This is the period which seems to be of most interest to modelers and railfan readers today as well as to the general public, because it represents the last era when the railroads were a dominant force in transportation.

Those interested in the B&O should find this volume a good representation of how it was on that road in its last era of high operation.

Thomas W. Dixon, Jr.
Lynchburg, Va., April 2011

Often-photographed daylight Mail & Express Train No. 29 is seen leaving Grafton with an F7AB set in October 1954, as Mikado (2-8-2) 4412 and 0-8-0 switcher 620, both probably having recently been removed from service as B&O steadily dieselized in this period. With a peak population of 8,500 in 1920, Grafton was very similar to Hinton on the C&O far to the south, with its coal operations and through mainline service. As Hinton was tied directly to C&O, so Grafton's life was tied directly to B&O. (Howard Barr, Sr. Photo)

1: Introduction

The Baltimore & Ohio, the nation's first common-carrier railroad, was chartered in Baltimore, Md., in 1827 because merchants in that port were looking for a way to increase inland trade with the West. They were attempting to take advantage of the fact that their city was on Chesapeake Bay to capture a sizable share of business at the expense of New York and Philadelphia, which relied on canals for their western trade.

Politics became the company's first obstacle. Neither Pennsylvania nor Virginia wanted a railroad that would carry products from their states to markets in a Maryland city. But when Pennsylvania chartered the Connellsville Railroad, Virginia apparently saw that it was about to get left behind and granted B&O permission to cross its territory. Construction began on July 4, 1828, and continued to Ellicotts Mills, Md., where the first 13-mile section of the railroad opened for business on May 24, 1830.

There was talk about connecting the railroad with the Chesapeake & Ohio Canal in the Potomac River Valley 50 miles west of Baltimore. But after the canal company tried unsuccessfully to keep B&O from purchasing property along the Potomac River, construction continued westward. Tracks reached the Potomac at Point of Rocks, Md., and ran next to the canal to a point on the Maryland-Virginia border across the river from Harpers Ferry, Va., with service starting on December 1, 1834 — nearly three decades before that part of the Old Dominion became West Virginia.

In January 1837, trains began to roll across an 800-foot covered wooden bridge onto Virginia soil, and soon were interchanging cars with the newly completed 32-mile Winchester & Potomac. B&O tracks now ran 81 miles from Baltimore to Harpers Ferry. The latter town served as the railroad's terminal until 1838, when Virginia amended the carrier's charter to permit it to extend itself to Cumberland, Md., and Wheeling, Va., on the Ohio River.

The river, of course, was merely the railroad founders' first goal, and grander schemes eventually formed in their minds because both St. Louis and New Orleans, located on the Mississippi River, offered opportunities for more traffic to and from the West and the South. But, for the time being, both the railroad and the canal company built toward Cumberland to connect with the National Road. That primitive but potentially prosperous pike, which catered to wagon and stagecoach traffic, had been launched in Cumberland in 1811, had reached Wheeling in 1818 and would eventually extend to Vandalia, Ill., in 1838.

Wheeling, which was entangled in a rivalry with Pittsburgh to be the head of navigation on the Ohio, had acquired a new importance with the arrival of the National Road, which permitted the transfer of goods between wagons from the East with boats from the West. In fact, Congress made Wheeling a port of entry in 1831, complete with customs facilities.

After the B&O reached Cumberland in 1842, it constructed a large yard and engine terminal to facilitate interchanges between the railroad and the National Road, while continuing to extend itself westward. By the end of 1852, tracks had reached Grafton, Fairmont and Wheeling.

The railroad's second challenge was the Allegheny Mountains. Stiff grades presented tremendous obstacles to the company's civil engineers, but they did well

One word that would describe the essence of the B&O, the nation's first common-carrier railroad, is "historic." This photo illustrates the point. Adapted from an old stereo slide, it shows 4-4-0 No. 17 at Harpers Ferry in 1860. (Photo from TLC Collection)

with the hand they were dealt. They not only over-came a 397-foot difference in elevation between Cumberland and Grafton, but also solved the problem of cresting a 2,628-foot summit at Altamont, Md., by having the track follow the North Branch of the Potomac River, the Savage and Cheat rivers, and several creeks.

The struggle started at Piedmont, located at the base of Backbone Mountain, with a 17-mile climb to Altamont, hence the name Seventeen Mile Grade. The steepest part of the grade was 2.29 percent. A gentle 1 percent descent to Terra Alta, W.Va., followed, but the western slope of Backbone Mountain required a drop of 2.67 percent at the steepest point on the next 11 miles into Rowlesburg, W.Va. This segment was called Cranberry Grade, named for the bogs located in the area.

From Rowlesburg, another stiff 2.06 percent climb began up Cheat Mountain for 5.2 miles to Tunnelton, but trains didn't have to reach all the way to the summit thanks to Kingwood Tunnel. Finally, westward trains descended on the 2.28 percent, 7.8-mile Newburg Grade to Hardman, after which trains negotiated the remaining few miles to Grafton easily.

With such grades providing formidable obstacles for loaded trains, helper stations were established at Hardman, Rowlesburg and Keyser. Hardman's helpers pushed eastbound trains up Newberg Grade and Keyser's helpers shoved westbound trains up Seventeen Mile Grade. Rowlesburg's M&K Junction was busy indeed; its helpers shoved loaded trains eastbound up Cranberry Grade and westbound up Cheat River Grade, and crews based there handled interchange traffic with the Morgantown & Kingwood Railroad — later a B&O branch — as well.

The carrier's third problem was the Ohio River itself. Wheeling had provided another connection with the National Road, but officers deemed the city unsuitable as a Western terminus because the upper Ohio River often was too low to allow access by packet boats. Even before it was finished, the "Old Main Line" was destined to become a mere branch when the B&O-backed Northwestern Virginia Railroad set out from Grafton to Parkersburg, a small river settlement nearly 100 miles below Wheeling. The Ohio was wider at that point and the railroad was more directly pointed toward the Midwest.

Traffic to Parkersburg began in 1857, and connections were established all the way to Cincinnati and St. Louis by way of the Marietta & Cincinnati and the Ohio & Mississippi railroads — both later taken into the B&O. At both Wheeling and Parkers-burg, ferries carried freight and passengers across the Ohio until bridges were completed in 1871.

The company operated a grand excursion in June 1857 to celebrate the Baltimore–St. Louis route, described in great detail the following year by B&O Master of Transportation William Prescott Smith. Dozens of notables went along for the ride, including U.S. Secretary of State Lewis Cass and M. de Sartiges, French minister plenipotentiary in Washington, D.C. Smith wrote that when the westward special, which left Baltimore's Camden Station at 6 a.m. on June 1, arrived at Piedmont, it was split into two trains for the assault on the mountains, and several passengers and members of the press climbed onto the engines for a bird's-eye view of the scenery as far as Altamont.

"One who has never ridden the iron horse can scarcely conceive the sensations produced thereby, nor can they be well described," Smith wrote. He told of seeing no signs of civilization "except one or two log houses and garden patches perched way up on the very summit of a peak, and occupied by some recluse who makes his living by hunting deer during the winter, and in the summer cultivates a little field of corn and potatoes for amusement merely."

At the first overnight stop in Grafton, the railroad's new hotel provided enough accommodations for the ladies and the most elderly gentlemen, but the other passengers had to snooze on the rudimentary sleepers of the day spotted on nearby yard tracks.

The exuberance of that moment came to an abrupt halt when the nation was plunged into the Civil War in 1861 — the conflict that gave birth to West Virginia two years later. B&O virtually straddled the boundary between North and South and provided the nation's capital with its only outlet to the North. Both sides tried alternately to use the company's tracks and destroy them, and a long period of recovery followed the four-year war.

Part of that recovery included the construction of a yard, car shop, and locomotive facilities in Keyser, W.Va., in 1872 to provide servicing for engines that faced the westbound climb up the mountains, repair of freight cars, and the easing of congestion in the Cumberland yard by classifying eastbound coal trains. During the remainder of the 19th century and the beginning years of the 20th, B&O continued to expand its presence in Northern West Virginia by building or acquiring several other routes — among them the Grafton & Belington; West Virginia & Pittsburgh (Clarksburg-Richwood and

Weston-Buckhannon-Pickens); Coal & Coke (Elkins-Charleston); Fairmont, Morgantown & Pittsburgh (Fairmont, W.Va., to Connellsville, Pa.); Hempfield (Wheeling, W.Va., to Washington, Pa.); Ohio River (Benwood-Kenova) and its affiliated West Virginia Short Line (Clarksburg-New Martinsville); Monongahela River (Clarksburg-Fairmont); and Winchester & Potomac. The B&O eventually extended the latter line into Lexington, Va., in an unsuccessful attempt to open for itself a southern gateway.

By the end of World War II, B&O owned and operated 36 percent of the 3,800 railroad route miles in West Virginia. The company hauled all kinds of mixed freight through the state as it passed between the Northeast and Midwest. But the principal product generated within the state clearly was coal. Hundreds of millions of tons of the mineral extracted from Mountain State mines were carried to electric generating plants, steel manufacturing centers and export piers over the years.

The carrier also developed a flourishing passenger business. At one time, people living in nearly every city and town in the northern and central parts of West Virginia could board B&O trains for family vacations and business trips. Added to this were the through streamliners running between the Jersey shore opposite New York City in the East and Chicago, Detroit, Cincinnati and St. Louis in the Midwest.

But sadly, after the war, the company's fortunes began to tumble. The recession of 1958 hit hard, and in 1961 the company lost $31 million. It sought refuge under the much stronger financial tent of the Chesapeake & Ohio Railway, and formal affiliation took place on February 4, 1963.

By the time B&O was officially dissolved into CSX

Transportation in 1987, both the "Old Main Line" between Fairmont and Moundsville and the "New Main Line" between Clarksburg and Parkersburg were gone, but trainloads of coal, chemicals and merchandise still rumbled across remaining routes, contributing significantly to the successor company's bottom line.

Another word that defines the B&O, at least in West Virginia, is "coal." We must confess that we don't know the location or owner of this mine, but it's clearly one of B&O's customers and is typical of scores of others throughout the system. (Photo from TLC Collection)

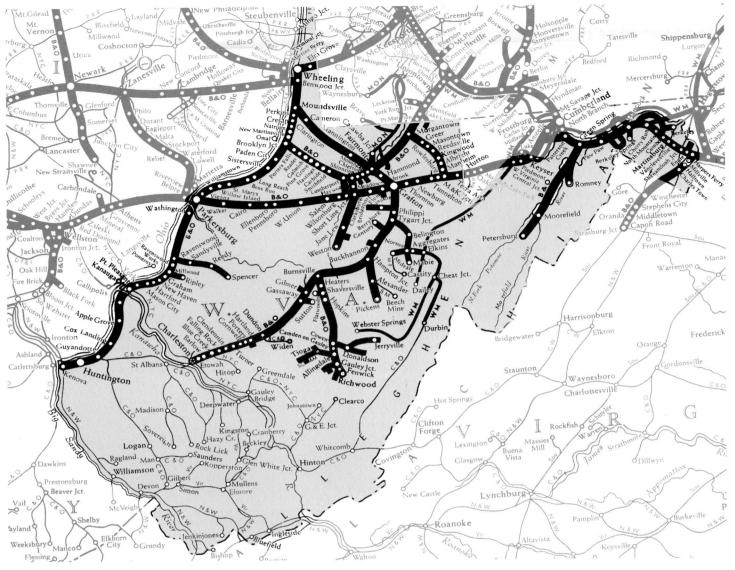

Class Q-4b Mikado 445 – it was a "MacArthur" to B&O after World War II in honor of Gen. Douglas MacArthur – simmers at the Benwood Junction shop on July 16, 1957. B&O had 135 of the heavy USRA-designed Mikes built by Baldwin in 1921-23. This one, which was known as 4468 until the renumbering of late 1956, has a meaningful claim to fame – it is the only Q-4 ever seen by the author, a few days later, in Parkersburg. it was officially retired in March 1958. (John Rehor photo, TLC Collection)

2: The Cumberland Division

The Baltimore & Ohio had taken more than seven years from its charter date to reach what would become West Virginia, but after a two-year hiatus construction of another 97 miles to Cumberland, Md., took only three years at a cost of $3.6 million. Tracks, which generally followed easy gradients along the Potomac River and its North Branch, reached Martinsburg in May 1842 and Cumberland the following November. They took another 10 years and another 99 mountainous miles to reach Grafton.

Subscribing to the philosophy that the original line could be built quickly and improved upon as time went on, the company double- and triple-tracked some segments of its main lines and built "cutoffs" to divert trains around trouble spots as it grew the business. Beginning in 1903, a 15-mile-long single-track detour known as the Cherry Run & Potomac Branch, or more commonly "the low line," diverged from the main lines at the community of Cumbo in order to bypass North Mountain and returned to the main lines at Miller Tower, just west of Cherry Run.

The 6.3-mile Patterson Creek Cutoff — which relieved freight congestion in Cumberland, Md., by avoiding the city altogether and shaved precious minutes from many passenger schedules — opened a year later.

The impressive 13.2-mile Magnolia Cutoff, which straightened out several kinks in the original main line along the twisting bank of the Potomac — was opened in 1914 between the small Eastern Panhandle communities of Orleans Road and Okonoko. Trains were getting longer and heavier, and this diversion eliminated a helper district over a 0.8 percent eastbound grade at Hansrote that was requiring those trains to tie up the original route while waiting for assistance. Besides, the cutoff provided an easier eastbound grade of 0.48 percent and more room for multiple tracks, which could not be fitted between the river and the hills on the original line.

The Cumberland Division had a split personality. Its eastern half featured easy grades and heavy traffic – the latter circumstance because it acted as a funnel handling traffic between the East Coast and both the Chicago and St. Louis lines. The western half carried fewer trains but presented tougher challenges because of its mountain grades. (Bob Withers Collection)

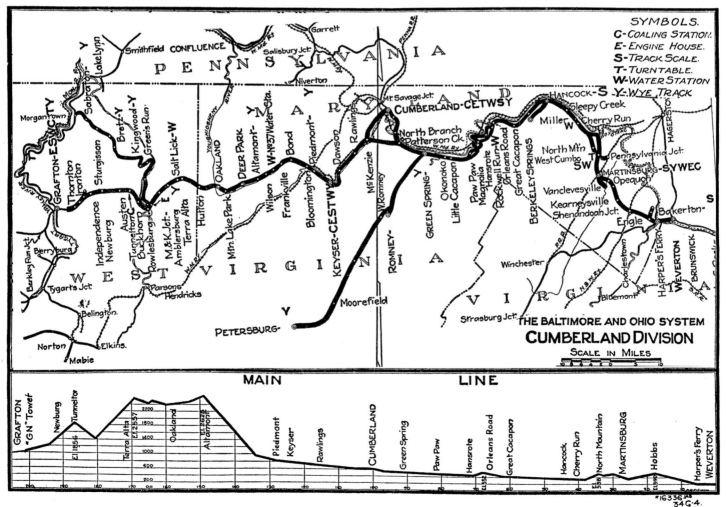

President Daniel Willard championed the $5.5 million project, which required building four double-tracked tunnels and two high bridges across the Potomac, removing a mountain, burrowing a deep cut, and constructing two massive concrete retaining walls measuring 1,800 feet and 3,100 feet in length.

Trains using the Magnolia Cutoff crossed the West Virginia/Maryland state line seven times before staying put in the Mountain State. The 1,592-foot-long Graham Tunnel, one of the cutoff's four new bores, was located between Magnolia and Kessler's Bridge, W.Va., and provided a topographical oddity. It was positioned at a point where the river — and a parcel of Maryland land — dipped south of the right of way. Thus, at the right moment, a long freight train's engines and caboose would be in West Virginia and the cars in the middle of the consist would be in Maryland.

The old line remained in service for years, playing host to most passenger trains and slow freights, but — like the Patterson Creek Cutoff — it eventually was abandoned.

Several branch lines sprouted from the Cumberland Division main or were acquired by the company, too. Among them were:

- The aforementioned Winchester & Potomac in 1870, which B&O extended — by financing new construction and arranging operating rights with another carrier — down to Lexington, Va., by 1883. Once the dream of a route to the South evaporated, several miles of that branch were abandoned.

- The 16-mile South Branch Railroad from Green Spring to Romney in 1884, which the parent road acquired to provide timber for its sprawling tie plant at Green Spring. B&O also bought the Hampshire Southern Railroad, which was completed from Romney Junction to Petersburg in 1910 and added another 36 miles to the branch. Today, this 52-mile line is owned by the state of West Virginia and is home to the popular Potomac Eagle excursion trains.

- The 6.1-mile line from Hancock to Berkeley Springs in 1888, which accessed the healing wa-

It seems like someone should hold a "Welcome to West Virginia" sign in front of the camera – one can almost see the point of the Mountain State's Eastern Panhandle in this photo of the Valley Local on the old Winchester & Potomac Branch – consisting of a motor car and trailer – connecting with an eastbound main line passenger train at Harpers Ferry in the 1920s. (B&O RR Historical Society Collection)

ters advertised by perhaps one of the oldest resorts in the country and was used to transport a high-quality sand useful in manufacturing glass.

• In 1920, B&O purchased the Morgantown & Kingwood Railroad, which was completed from Morgantown to Rowlesburg in 1907 by connecting with an older two-mile branch from the latter point, to access the several coal mines it served. Later, its midsection was abandoned and each remnant was reached from its original end points.

The branches contributed much revenue to the company, but, by far, most of the money that flowed into B&O coffers from the Cumberland Division came from eastbound coal, "Quick Delivery" freight running in both directions, and the company's fleet of passenger trains running between Jersey City, N.J., Washington and St. Louis.

One of B&O's first three four-unit sets of Class FT freight locomotives rumbles across the Harpers Ferry bridge with a trainload of oil during World War II as a dynamometer car monitors the units' performance. General Motors' Electro Motive Division built the 5,400-horsepower sets in 1942, when their just-invented dynamic braking was all the rage. (TLC Collection)

This post card, postmarked in 1909, shows the Harpers Ferry station and waiting shed for westbound passengers as the camera is pointed back toward Maryland. The station and shed still stand, serving Maryland Area Rail Commuter passenger trains, but the tower that was once a part of the station is long gone. (TLC Collection)

A B&O 2-10-2 thunders across the Harpers Ferry bridge with a 91-car westbound Timesaver at 12:23 p.m. on a chilly March 3, 1947. (Bruce D. Fales photo, Jay Williams Collection)

A Class Q-4b MacArthur carries more westbound mixed freight across the Harpers Ferry bridge in this undated photo. Note the auxiliary water tank. (Bert Pennypacker photo, TLC Collection)

A "racetrack special" made up of Budd RDC cars heads down the Winchester Branch for Charlestown at Harpers Ferry on Aug. 13, 1966. (Railroad Avenue Enterprises)

The Potomac and Shenandoah rivers, the bluff on the Maryland shore, the western portal of Harpers Ferry tunnel, and even the traffic mix is still the same; only the date has changed. A three-unit diesel headed by F7 No. 4597 advances westbound freight into West Virginia at Harpers Ferry in October 1974. (Ron Piskor photo, TLC Collection)

Coal is the dominant – in fact, the only – lading in view in this undated company photograph taken east of Martinsburg. (B&O Railroad Museum Collection)

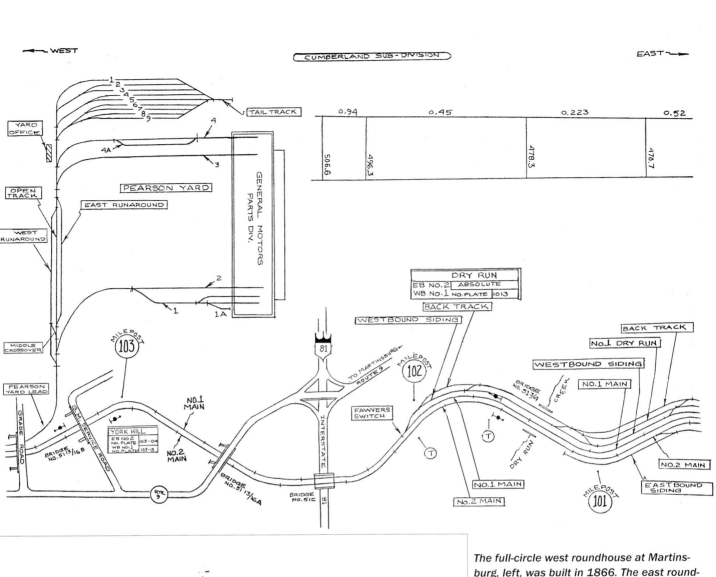

The full-circle west roundhouse at Martinsburg, left, was built in 1866. The east roundhouse, below, was built six years later and gutted by a fire set by juveniles in 1990. (TLC Collection)

Several locomotives congregate around the Martinsburg shops in this undated photo, showing that the city's yard, although fairly small, is busy. (Hicks Collection, B&O RR Historical Society archive)

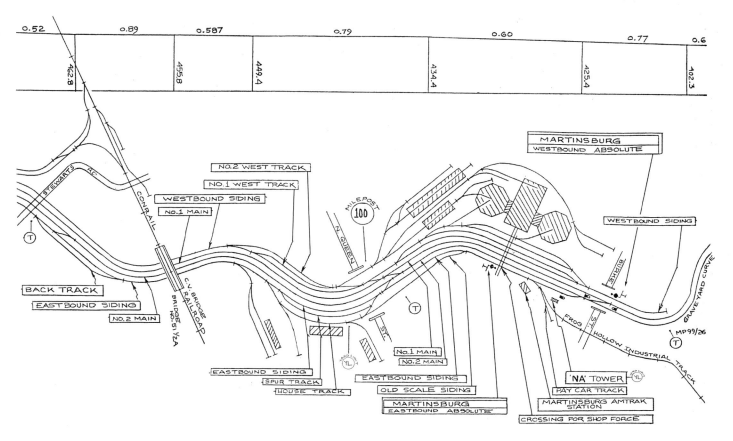

This map reveals that the Martinsburg Yard seems to be arranged on a more curvy alignment than the easy grades of the eastern Cumberland Division would require. (Bernie Beavers map, B&O RR Historical Society publication)

Class E-19 2-8-0 Camelback No. 1796 works at Martinsburg in May 1930. Baldwin built the locomotive in June 1901 and it is two years away from retirement. (TLC Collection)

One of the locomotives based at Martinsburg on July 25, 1948, is Class Q-1aa MacArthur 4014. Baldwin built it in February 1911. It will face the scrapper's torch in February 1950. (Howard Ameling photo, TLC Collection)

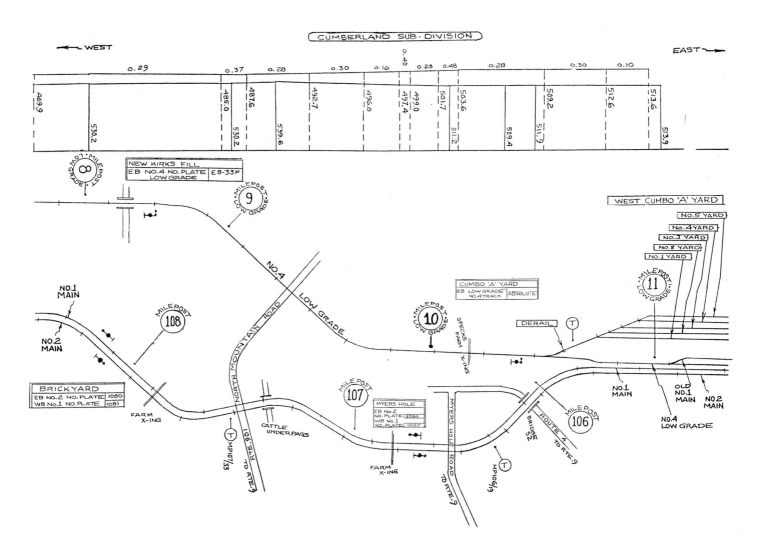

◄── WEST   EAST ──►

Distances: 0.29   0.37   0.28   0.30   0.16   0.40   0.23   0.48   0.28   0.30   0.10

Mileposts (top): 469.9   530.2   485.0   487.6   539.6   492.7   496.0   497.4   499.0   511.2   501.7   503.6   509.4   509.2   511.9   512.6   513.6   513.9

MILEPOST 8   LOW GRADE

NEW KIRKS FILL
EB NO.4	NO. PLATE	E8-33F
LOW GRADE		

MILEPOST 9   LOW GRADE

WEST CUMBO 'A' YARD

NO.5 YARD
NO.4 YARD
NO.3 YARD
NO.2 YARD
NO.1 YARD

NO.4 LOW GRADE

NO.1 MAIN

NO.2 MAIN

MILEPOST 108

CUMBO 'A' YARD
EB LOW GRADE	NO.4 TRACK	ABSOLUTE

MILEPOST 10   LOW GRADE

MILEPOST 11   LOW GRADE

SPECKS FARM X-ING

DERAIL   (T)

BRICKYARD
EB NO.2	NO.PLATE	1080
WB No.1	NO.PLATE	1081

FARM X-ING

CATTLE UNDERPASS

NORTH MOUNTAIN ROAD

(T) MP107/33   RTE.9 107/06

MILEPOST 107

MYERS HOLE
EB No.2		
NO. PLATE	1086	
WB No.1		
NO. PLATE	1087	

MYERS HOLE ROAD   TO RTE.9

FARM X-ING

(T)   MP106/19

BRIDGE 52

MILEPOST 106

ROUTE 9 TO RTE.9

NO.1 MAIN

OLD NO.1 MAIN

NO.2 MAIN

NO.4 LOW GRADE

An operator is gainfully occupied at HO Tower in Hancock in this July 1931 photo. The tower was opened in 1901 and updated in 1912. For a long while, it stood at the point where three main tracks became four. (B&O RR Historical Society Collection)

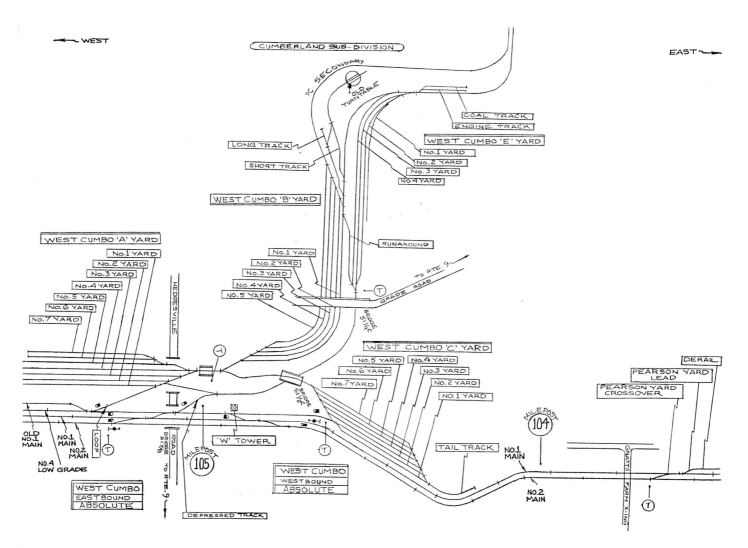

The yards at Cumbo and West Cumbo – not to be confused with Cumberland, which is in Maryland – were constructed in a remote section of Berkeley County between 1909 and 1915 to handle vast tonnages exchanged between B&O and the PRR-controlled Cumberland Valley Railroad. PRR also controlled B&O at the time and, wishing to thwart George Gould's plans for a transcontinental railroad empire, ordered that eastbound B&O tonnage formerly handed to the Gould-controlled Western Maryland at Cherry Run remain on B&O tracks and be handed over to the CV at West Cumbo. By 1927, B&O was free from PRR domination and also controlled WM – so the interchange point reverted to Cherry Run. But even with the loss of much of its traffic, West Cumbo remained a major facility into the 1980s. (Bernie Beavers map, B&O RR Historical Society publications)

The handsome little station in Berkeley Springs, at the end of a 6.1-mile branch from Hancock, was built in 1915 to greet suffering passengers flocking to the town's healing waters. All too soon, the company replaced steam-powered passenger trains with a gas motor car and trailer that still made three daily trips to connect with main line trains into the 1930s. (TLC Collection)

<— WEST　　　　　　(CUMBERLAND SUB-DIVISION)　　　　　　EAST —>

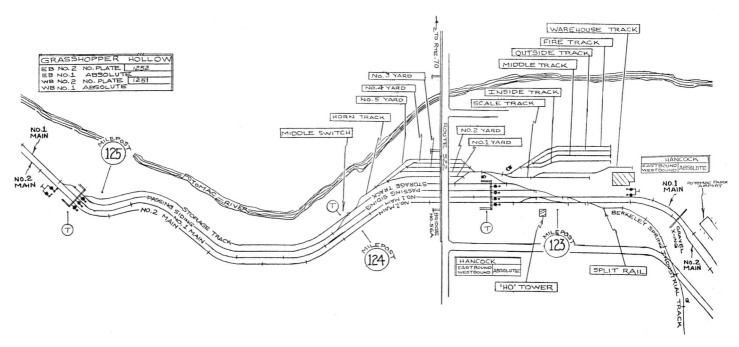

0.30	0.15	0.08	0.20	0.06	0.09	0.36	0.11	0.09	0.04	0.30	0.22	0.14
422.3	416.8	417.5	420.3	419.3	417.5	420.8	421.3		420.4	421.1	418.7	411.9

GRASSHOPPER HOLLOW

EB NO.2	NO. PLATE	1252
EB NO.1	ABSOLUTE	
WB NO.2	NO. PLATE	1251
WB NO.1	ABSOLUTE	

By the time this diagram was drawn in the late 1980s, the Hancock Yard was less busy than in the good ol' days – but still served several local customers. (Bernie Beavers map, B&O RR Historical Society publications)

Class S-1a 2-10-2 No. 6211 charges toward Round Top with Chicago 97 in 1940. Many B&O engineers said the big, beefy Baldwins were the best steam engines ever built. (Bruce D. Fales photo, TLC Collection)

Class EM-1 2-8-8-4 No. 7624 throws a lot of smoke into the sky as it barrels along west of Sir John's Run with 59 cars of mixed freight on July 7, 1951. (Bruce D. Fales photo, Jay Williams Collection)

This company photograph, taken at the small community of Orleans Road near the eastern end of the Magnolia Cutoff ca. 1953 shows how busy this section of B&O's funnel is. It also reveals how sharply the eastern half of the Cumberland Division differs from its mountainous western half. (B&O photo, B&O RR Historical Society Collection)

An eastbound freight train traverses the original mainline ca. 1955, separated from the Magnolia Cutoff only by a massive concrete retaining wall. (B&O RR Historical Society Collection)

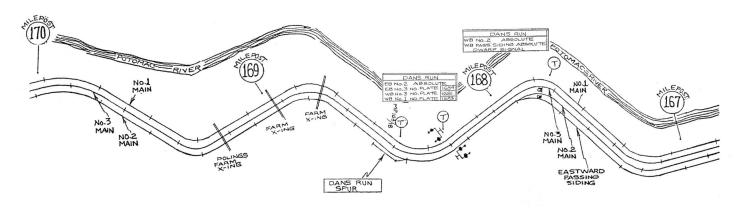

.19	0.01	0.26	0.00	0.15	0.08	0.12	0.18	0.00	0.17	0.24	0.10	0.11	0.15	0.14	0.14	0.07
569.8	569.7	571.3	571.3	569.7	569.0	570.5	568.5	568.5	567.2	568.4	567.7	569.1	567.0	568.1	567.0	

Green Spring has two claims to fame – it's the junction of a branch to Romney, Moorefield and Petersburg known today as the state-owned South Branch Valley Railroad – and it's the site of a tie treatment plant where creosote, zinc chloride and other chemicals were forced into crossties under pressure to lengthen their lives as they supported the rails and trains of the B&O system. Hence this yard, to support all that. (Bernie Beavers map, B&O RR Historical Society publication)

Class Q-3 MacArthur 4531 brings west-bound freight out of Carothers Tunnel on the Magnolia Cutoff near Little Cacapon in 1938. (Bruce D. Fales photo, TLC Collection)

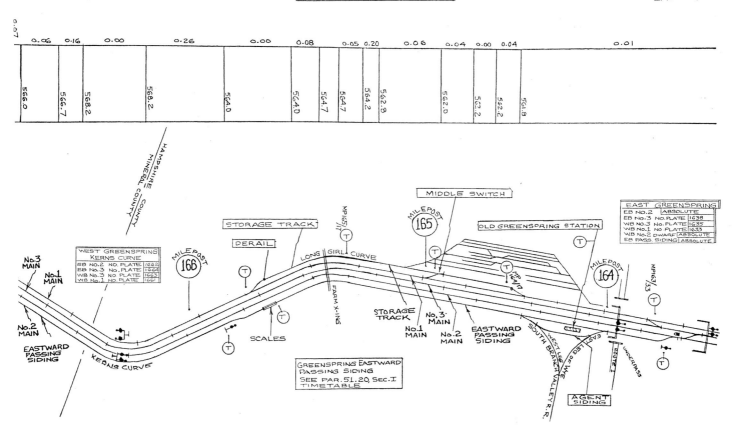

Class S-1a Santa Fe 6211 charges past Paw Paw on the Magnolia Cutoff with an eastbound coal train at 5:58 p.m. on Aug. 13, 1939. (Bruce D. Fales, Jay Williams Collection)

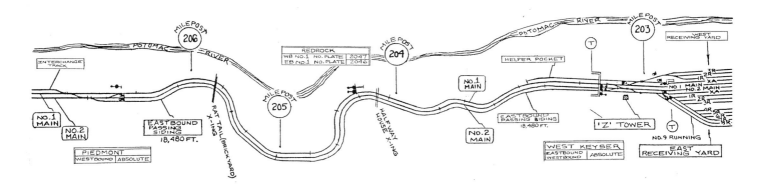

| 0.536 | | 0.34 | 0.63 | 0.458 | 0.81 | 0.15 | 0.44 | 0.51 | 0.38 | 0.06 | 0.30 | 0.84 | 0.30 | 0.37 | 0.234 |

| | 911.4 | 908.7 | 901.1 | | 882.8 | 877.9 | 876.9 | 868.5 | 859.3 | 855.4 | 855.0 | 852.3 | 849.0 | 847.3 | 839.7 |

◄—► SEVENTEEN MILE GRADE —►

Keyser's two-mile-long yard provided space to classify coal bound for eastern markets, which would then take the Patterson Creek Cutoff around Cumberland and avoid congestion there. Today, the yard is almost gone. (Bernie Beavers map, B&O RR Historical Society publication)

B&O's main line has crossed the line back into Maryland and entered the city of Cumberland, where it split – with one leg heading for Chicago and the other for St. Louis. Now, we are back in West Virginia on the St. Louis line, looking at the next large yard to the West at Keyser. It's obvious why the yard was constructed – coal. (B&O Railroad Museum Collection)

The station at Romney was built when the B&O-backed South Branch Railroad completed its line from Green Spring in 1884. Future B&O predecessor Hampshire Southern extended the branch to Moorefield and Petersburg in 1910. Today, the Potomac Eagle tourist trains operate on the route. (TLC Collection)

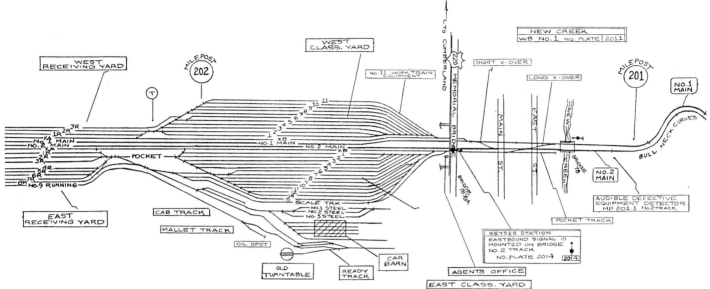

The station at Piedmont looks more like an old office building than a depot, but at least it appears to be doing a brisk business in this post card view. (TLC Collection)

A shop employee fills the sand dome of Class Q-4b MacArthur 4609 at Keyser in June 1944. (TLC Collection)

Either way, a tough climb

B&O faced formidable challenges in both directions on the 101.4-mile West End of the Cumberland Division, but most acutely with its huge eastbound coal traffic.

The West End basically consisted of four steep grades from west to east. The 2.28 percent, 7.8-mile Newburg Grade started at Hardman, which was a helper station 10 miles east of Grafton, and reached its summit inside Kingwood Tunnel between West End Tower and Tunnelton. Then, eastbound trains went down the 2.06 percent, six-mile Cheat River Grade to Rowlesburg before starting up the 2.67 percent, 11.9-mile Cranberry Grade to Terra Alta. From Terra Alta to Altamont, Md., eastbound coal and manifest trains had a comparatively easy time of it, basically descending on a roller-coaster profile until encountering a 1.04 percent, 6.2 mile climb from Mountain Lake Park, Md., to Altamont and the Allegheny summit 2,628 feet above sea level, which required helpers in steam days. Then they descended Seventeen Mile Grade to Piedmont, which averaged 2.18 percent and at times reached 2.29 percent. From there, it was only a 0.5 percent descent for five miles into Keyser.

So, whether struggling to lift tonnage on Newburg and Cranberry or keeping the trains under control on the Cheat River and Seventeen Mile grades, eastbound drags had a tough assignment indeed. Of course, lugging westbound manifest freights and empty hopper trains was no cinch, either. Passenger trains struggled in both directions, too.

In the all-steam era, Keyser dispatched westbound helpers on Seventeen Mile Grade, M&K Junction at Rowlesburg sent helpers west up Cheat River Grade and east up Cranberry Grade, and Hardman provided eastbound helpers for Newburg Grade. The standard for eastbound freights in this territory – where 65 cars made a train – was a plodding 2-8-8-0 up front and two more behind. The arrival of B&O's powerful EM-1 2-8-8-4's in 1944-45 permitted an increase in tonnage – but not by much. Eastbound passenger trains running from Grafton to Keyser or Cumberland needed a MacArthur and a Pacific or two MacArthurs up front and another Mike behind.

In the transition era when diesels powered passenger trains, westbound runs received front-end steam helpers at Cumberland or Keyser; they headed eastbound runs from Grafton. As diesels kept coming, a trio of F7 freight units usually replaced E-unit pairs altogether on passenger trains between Cumberland or Keyser and Grafton.

Once F7's arrived in force at M&K Junction in 1949, the changes accelerated. Hardman's engine facility was closed and all helpers on Cranberry, Cheat River and Newburg grades were headquartered at M&K Junction. That resulted in the retirement or reassignment of 19 articulateds, six MacArthurs, and one "Big Six" 2-10-2.

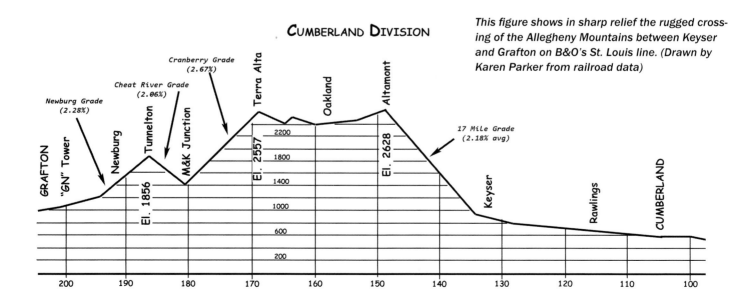

CUMBERLAND DIVISION

This figure shows in sharp relief the rugged crossing of the Allegheny Mountains between Keyser and Grafton on B&O's St. Louis line. (Drawn by Karen Parker from railroad data)

M&K became the base for 31 diesels – four four-unit helper sets, two spare F7 helpers, 12 F7's that worked other assignments, and a single SD9.

Flexibility was the name of the game once diesels were supreme. Three F7's on the front and four on the rear of eastbound freights was the standard. From M&K, helpers might be dispatched to Hardman to pick up an eastbound, cut off at Kingwood Tunnel and go back to Hardman for another eastbound – while their first train picked up another helper at M&K for the run up Cranberry. Or, the helpers might be told to follow the first eastbound to M&K on approach blocks and tie on again for Cranberry. Helpers returning from Terra Alta might boost another eastbound from M&K or be instructed to continue to Hardman for an eastbound. Eastbound Timesavers, competing with the fast freights of other carriers, always kept a set of helpers on the rear from Hardman to Terra Alta, saving a 10-minute stop at M&K.

Officers bragged that diesels – with their flat-maintaining air brakes and dynamics, which obviated the need to turn retainers on each car up and down on the summits and in the valleys – shaved more than two hours off the running time of eastbound freight trains from Grafton to Keyser.

Class Q-4 MacArthur 4445 has just disengaged from an eastbound freight train at Terra Alta, just east of the crest of Cranberry Grade, in June 1944. (TLC Collection)

The impressive dimensions of Salt Lick Curve are evident in this photo, where the complete train is visible. Note the water tank, which probably has slaked the thirst of many weary steam engines. (B&O photo, B&O RR Historical Society archive)

Above: Class EL-3a 2-8-8-0 No. 7204 and two helpers on the rear struggle to lift an eastbound coal train up Cranberry Grade west of Terra Alta on June 10, 1949. (W.H. Thrall photo, TLC Collection)

Opposite Top: Class EL-1a 7109 and Class EL-2 7202 help the engine up front, Class EL-5a 7169, lug a trainload of coal through Salt Lick Curve west of Terra Alta at 11:26 a.m. on June 12, 1949. Three 2-8-8-0's are required to haul 65 eastbound loads. (Bruce D. Fales photo, Jay Williams Collection)

Opposite Bottom: The photographer can't resist taking another photo of the helpers on the same drag as they pass closer to his vantage point. (Bruce D. Fales photo, Jay Williams Collection)

Eastbound helpers are nearly finished with another assignment as their train reaches the clearly visible crest of Cranberry Grade at Terra Alta on Oct. 21, 1945. (Bob's Photo Collection, B&O RR Historical Society archive)

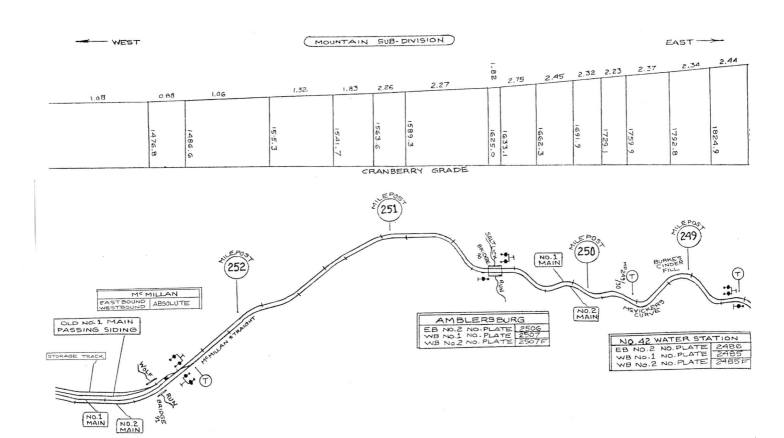

CRANBERRY GRADE

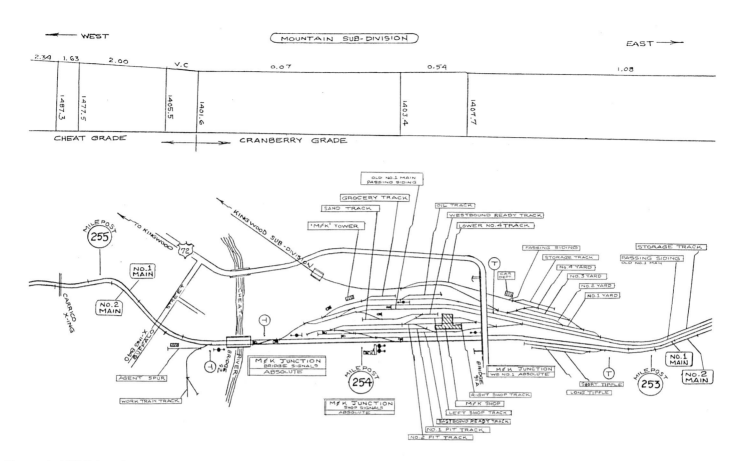

The yard at M&K Junction supported a locomotive servicing facility and enough tracks to collect coal and other commodities from the Morgantown & Kingwood Branch for forwarding on the main line. (Bernie Beavers map, B&O RR Historical Society publication)

Class EL-4 2-8-8-0 No. 7033 simmers between assignments at M&K Junction in June 1944. M&K's helpers shoved trains eastward on Cranberry Grade and westward on Cheat River Grade. (TLC Collection)

Opposite: The engineer aboard Class EM-1 2-8-8-4 No. 7622 has his locomotive exerting all 115,000 pounds of tractive effort as it and two articulated pushers which are out of sight advance an eastbound Timesaver over the steepest part of Cranberry Grade west of Terra Alta ca. 1947. (Bruce D. Fales photo, Jay Williams Collection)

Above: Class Q-1c MacArthur 4226 prances about among the mallets at M&K Junction in June 1944. The 2-8-2, which Baldwin built in 1913, likely is assigned to perform yard duties, make light helper runs or collect loads of coal on the M&K Branch. It will meet a fiery Waterloo scarcely a year later when its boiler explodes. (TLC Collection)

Opposite Top: It's 1950, and a Mallet rests at right in the M&K terminal. But note the four-unit F7 diesel helper in the distance at center. It and several identical units have been there since late summer 1949, and they eventually will empty M&K of steam by early 1953. (TLC Collection)

Opposite Bottom: Class EL-4 No. 7033 simmers at the M&K shop on the night of Sept. 28, 1948. The labor of assisting trains continued around the clock. On a typical day in 1945, the 14 mallets and six MacArthurs stationed at M&K handled 21 eastbound and 17 westbound shoves in addition to several passenger assignments and work on the M&K Subdivision. (Bruce D. Fales photo, Jay Williams Collection)

Class EM-1 No. 7605 charges out of M&K with westbound empties at 5:15 p.m. on Sept. 28, 1948. The company's massive 2-8-8-4's, just three and four years old, will last at M&K longer than their older cousins. (Bruce D. Fales photo, Jay Williams Collection)

Class Q-4 MacArthur 4422 and Class P-1d Pacific 5094 bring an eight-car Metropolitan Special, westbound Train 11, into Rowlesburg on June 29, 1947. (E.L. Thompson photo, B&O RR Historical Society Collection)

Class EL-3a 2-8-8-0 No. 7125 comes down the Cheat River Grade in Rowlesburg with a coal train on April 24, 1940. (Howard N. Barr Sr. photo, TLC Collection)

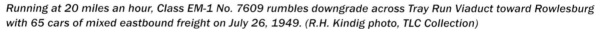

Running at 20 miles an hour, Class EM-1 No. 7609 rumbles downgrade across Tray Run Viaduct toward Rowlesburg with 65 cars of mixed eastbound freight on July 26, 1949. (R.H. Kindig photo, TLC Collection)

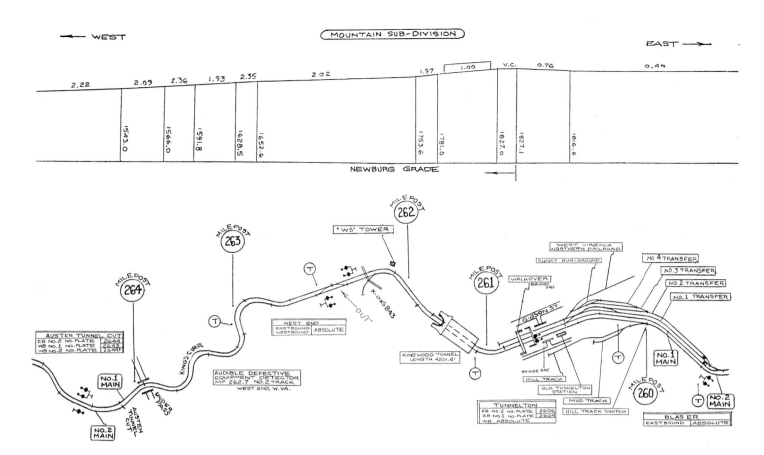

The yard at Blaser and Tunnelton, near the top of the Cheat River Grade, provided a gathering spot for yet more coal off the West Virginia Northern short line. Blaser was named for a B&O officer. (Bernie Beavers map, B&O RR Historical Society publication)

Class EL-5a 2-8-8-0 No. 7151 totes eastbound coal between Kingwood Tunnel and Tunnelton on June 11, 1949. (W.H. Thrall, TLC Collection)

Class EL-5a 2-8-8-0 No. 7170 is down to its knees at 5 miles an hour as it crawls up Newburg Grade at Austen with 54 loads of coal on July 27, 1949. (R.H. Kindig photo, TLC Collection)

Two 2-8-8-0 helpers, Class EL-5a 7153 and Class EL-3a 7133, do all they can to assist the 7170's train seen in the photo above, but they're still only making 5 miles an hour. (R.H. Kindig photo, TLC Collection)

Hardman, 10 miles east of Grafton at the foot of Newburg Grade, was a helper station in its own right for many years. Ten Mallets were assigned here unit 1949, when they were transferred to M&K Junction in preparation for the advent of diesel helpers. (TLC Collection)

3: The Monongah Division

Except for the Baltimore & Ohio's trackage across the Ohio River bridges at Wheeling and Parkersburg to Bellaire and Belpre, Ohio, the entire 1,140.8-mile Monongah Division was located inside West Virginia. The division hauled all kinds of freight — including chemicals, glassware, carbon products, gasoline, coke, steel, pottery, chinaware, sand, gravel, natural gas, and oil well equipment — but, clearly, it was the system's most productive generator of coal traffic. In 1950, bituminous coal accounted for 44 percent of all freight tonnage on the railroad, and 60 percent of that amount originated on the Monongah Division or lateral lines feeding it at connecting points. In summer 1951, a total of 175 trains operated daily over the division.

Beginning in 1941, B&O developed the Gauley coal field in a big way. The company rebuilt the Burnsville-Richwood and the leased Strouds Creek & Muddlety lines, signed an operating agreement with the Cherry River Boom & Lumber Co. at Richwood to haul coal mined on its line, extended branches, installed new track to connect existing lines in more efficient ways, lured mine operators to the territory to take advantage of mineral rights the company owned, and built an extensive classification yard at Cowen. Tonnage originating in the Gauley field grew from 14,000 in 1938 to more than 3 million in 1950.

The company also had to relocate the old Grafton & Belington line between Grafton and Berryburg Junction because of construction of the Tygart Valley Dam, so it also rehabilitated additional mileage to Burnsville to make a through heavy-duty route between Grafton and Cowen. A few little-used lines were abandoned, including Weston-Orlando (near Burnsville) and Weston-Buckhannon.

But much tonnage came from other Monongah Division territories as well. The system's largest and most productive mines were located within a 20-mile radius of Fairmont. The Northern West Virginia Coal Region also included mines at Lumberport and Dola on the West Virginia Short Line, between Clarksburg and Weston on the old West Virginia & Pittsburgh, on the main line from Clarksburg west to Wolf Summit and east to Grafton; and several more in the Elkins, Buckhannon and Clay County areas.

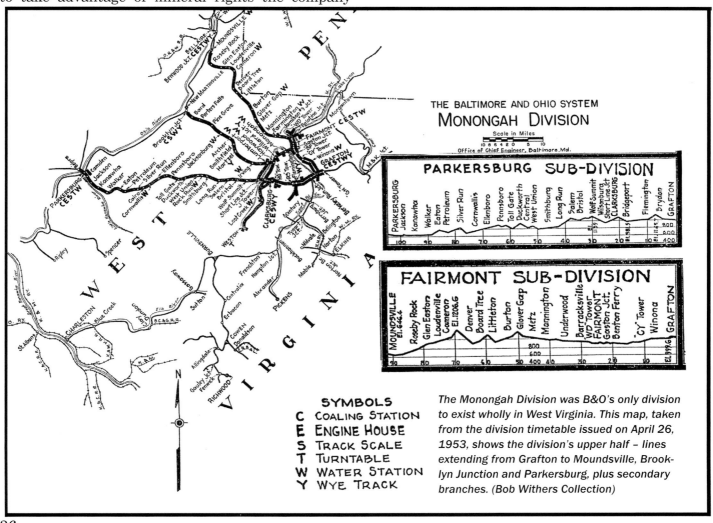

SYMBOLS
C COALING STATION
E ENGINE HOUSE
S TRACK SCALE
T TURNTABLE
W WATER STATION
Y WYE TRACK

The Monongah Division was B&O's only division to exist wholly in West Virginia. This map, taken from the division timetable issued on April 26, 1953, shows the division's upper half – lines extending from Grafton to Moundsville, Brooklyn Junction and Parkersburg, plus secondary branches. (Bob Withers Collection)

Standard operating practice when B&O doubleheaded locomotives was to place the lighter engine ahead of the heavier, as seen here. United States Railroad Administration-designed Class Q-3 light MacArthur 4502 (Baldwin, 1918) leads Class Q-4b heavy MacArthur 4473 (Baldwin, 1922) out of Grafton in October 1955 with 122 cars of westbound freight. (Herbert H. Harwood Jr. Collection)

Westbound Class Q-3 light MacArthurs 4526 and 4576 pass the Grafton passenger station on their way out of town on Aug. 5, 1953 – likely heading for Cowen. (W.E. Hopkins photo, Bob Withers Collection)

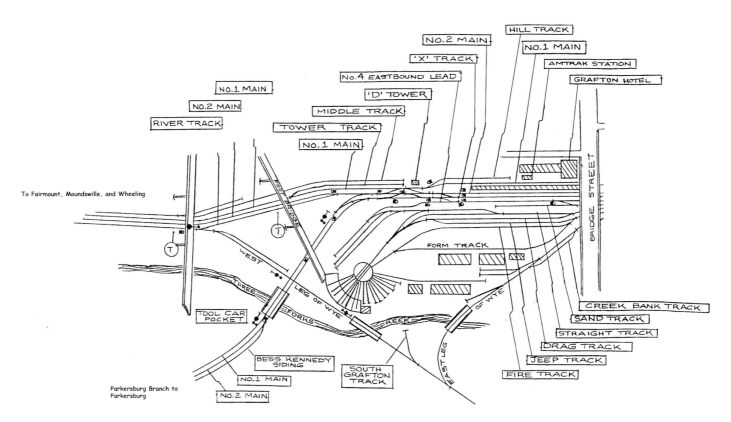

NO.1 MAIN

NO.2 MAIN

RIVER TRACK

TOWER TRACK

MIDDLE TRACK

NO.1 MAIN

'D' TOWER

NO.4 EASTBOUND LEAD

'X' TRACK

NO.2 MAIN

HILL TRACK

NO.1 MAIN

AMTRAK STATION

GRAFTON HOTEL

BRIDGE STREET

FORM TRACK

To Fairmount, Moundsville, and Wheeling

WEST

FOOT BRIDGE

THREE FORKS

LEG OF WYE

CREEK

EAST LEG OF WYE

TOOL CAR POCKET

BESS KENNEDY SIDING

NO.1 MAIN

NO.2 MAIN

SOUTH GRAFTON TRACK

Parkersburg Branch to Parkersburg

CREEK BANK TRACK

SAND TRACK

STRAIGHT TRACK

DRAG TRACK

JEEP TRACK

FIRE TRACK

You could never tell it from its long, large yard, but Grafton actually was a small town. It was the quintessential railroad town – planned and built to meet the company's needs and be populated by the company's labor force. (Bernie Beavers map, B&O RR Historical Society publication)

Opposite Below: If an EPA inspector were to visit Grafton's smoky engine terminal in 1947 as the photographer did, he would likely have gone mad. Railfans, on the other hand, would have been in hog heaven. (E.L. Thompson photo, B&O RR Historical Society archive)

Below: Adding to the noxious air at the Grafton engine terminal in the late 1940s was this Class EM-1 2-8-8-4, sending its two cents' worth of pollutants aloft with the best of them during its short life. (TLC Collection)

Class Q-4b MacArthur 4618 takes a breather in the Grafton servicing facility in August 1954. (W.E. Hopkins photo, Bob Withers Collection)

For all too brief a while, Grafton offered aspiring rail photographers a wide variety of steam engine types. This is Class Q-7f MacArthur 4855 resting between assignments on Aug. 5, 1953. Baldwin built the locomotive in 1916 and B&O would sell it for scrap in August 1954. (W.E. Hopkins photo, Bob Withers Collection)

Class L-2 0-8-0 switcher 1611 awaits its next assignment in front of Grafton's massive coal dock in August 1954. (W.E. Hopkins photo, Bob Withers Collection)

Passenger power was evident in big numbers, too, at Grafton's engine servicing facilities. Here, Class P-1c Pacific 5045 simmers on Aug. 5, 1953. (W.E. Hopkins photo, Bob Withers Collection)

Class E-27ca Consolidation 2755 prances about in the Grafton yard on a rainy day in July 1954. (W.E. Hopkins photo, Bob Withers Collection)

Wreck crane X217 and tender X1044 await their next call in Grafton on Oct. 25, 1955. At 250 tons' capacity, the X217 is among the heaviest diesel-powered cranes on the system. (TLC Collection)

Class P-1c Pacific 5002 takes Train 65 out of Grafton on Aug. 8, 1951, heading for Fairmont and Morgantown in West Virginia and Connellsville in Pennsylvania. The branch-line passenger run includes five regular cars and two deadheading sleepers. (E.L. Thompson photo, B&O RR Historical Society Collection)

A Class EM-1 2-8-8-4 and caboose head toward Haywood and Lumberport at Gaston Junction, near Fairmont, in August 1947. The line from Grafton passes in front of the train order office, which is known as JC Tower even though it is a single-story building. (O.V. Nelson photo, Bob Withers Collection)

Class EM-1 2-8-8-4 No. 669 (numbered 7619 until late 1956) rests between runs at the Fairmont engine terminal on Sept. 6, 1957. The giant articulateds moved a lot of coal from Fairmont to Benwood and on to the Lake Erie docks after diesels bumped them from the main lines. Sadly, this fine engine went to scrap a year later. (Theodore F. Gleichmann Jr. photo, B&O RR Historical Society archive)

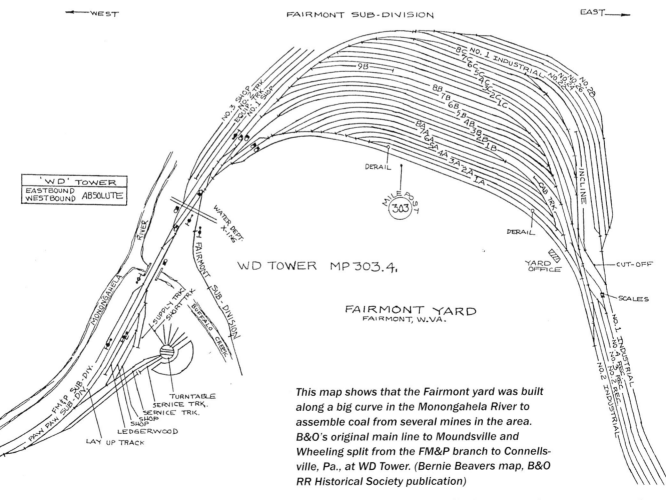

This map shows that the Fairmont yard was built along a big curve in the Monongahela River to assemble coal from several mines in the area. B&O's original main line to Moundsville and Wheeling split from the FM&P branch to Connellsville, Pa., at WD Tower. (Bernie Beavers map, B&O RR Historical Society publication)

The Fairmont passenger station is bereft of passengers and trains in this June 1958 photo. It was torn down soon after. The last trains to call here were Wheeling-Grafton Nos. 440/343-441/344, which made their last trips in October 1957. The complicated numbers derive from the fact that the trains reversed timetable direction at Moundsville. (O.V. Nelson photo, Bob Withers Collection)

Engineer Glen Hardman, at the controls of Class P-1d Pacific 5068, has brought Train 343 into Fairmont at 6:25 on an August 1948 morning. While conductor Harry L. Dawson (not shown) greets passengers, fireman C.A. Clark fills the locomotive's water tank. A work train is in the siding at left and cars on Walker siding are ready to be unloaded at right. (O.V. Nelson photo, Bob Withers Collection)

Jamison No. 8 mine tipple at Farmington, owned by the Jamison Coal & Coke Co. in Greensburg, Pa., is typical of the mining operations along B&O's original main line. In 1937, the mine produced 60 daily carloads in 10 different sizes of coal – from pulverized to lump. (B&O Coals: 1937 Handbook & Directory of Coal Mines & Coke Ovens served by The Baltimore & Ohio Railroad, published by the Coal Information Bureau Inc., TLC Collection)

Less than five miles up the mine from Jamison No. 8 and 9 tipples was Rachel Mine, owned by Jones Colleries Inc. of Pittsburgh. In 1937, the mine produced eight different sizes of coal with a daily output of 40 cars. (B&O Coals: 1937 Handbook & Directory of Coal Mines & Coke Ovens served by The Baltimore & Ohio Railroad, published by the Coal Information Bureau Inc., TLC Collection)

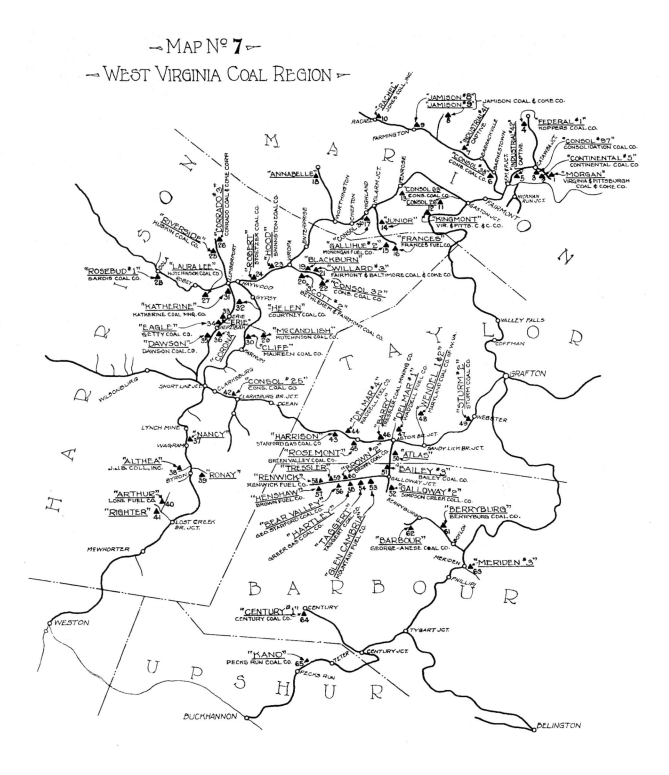

This map locates the 65 mines B&O served in the "West Virginia Coal Region" in 1937. (B&O Coals: 1937 Handbook & Directory of Coal Mines & Coke Ovens served by The Baltimore & Ohio Railroad, published by the Coal Information Bureau Inc., TLC Collection)

Class Q-1aa MacArthur 4041 – on its first trip after a rebuild at the Fairmont shop –passes under the U.S. 19 bridge as it approaches the city with 90 loads of coal from mines at Barrackville, Farmington and Rachel in March 1948. The engineer is C.M. Rush and the fireman is G.W. Mills. Buffalo Creek is unusually high after heavy rains. (O.V. Nelson photo, Bob Withers Collection)

Several people are awaiting a train at Mannington in this post card photo. The post card was postmarked in 1907. (TLC Collection)

B. AND O. DEPOT, MANNINGTON, W. VA.,

Train 343 exits Sales Tunnel near Hundred on its way to Wheeling on the morning of May 1, 1953. Trains 343 and 344 carried a 10-section/2-compartment/drawing room Washington, D.C.-Wheeling sleeper, which was handled by Trains 23 and 24 east of Grafton. The eastbound car was carried on Train 18 east of Cumberland, Md. (O.V. Nelson photo, Bob Withers Collection)

This post card, which was postmarked in 1913, shows the handsome station at Cameron, the westernmost regular stop for Trains 343 and 344 on the Monongah Division. (TLC Collection)

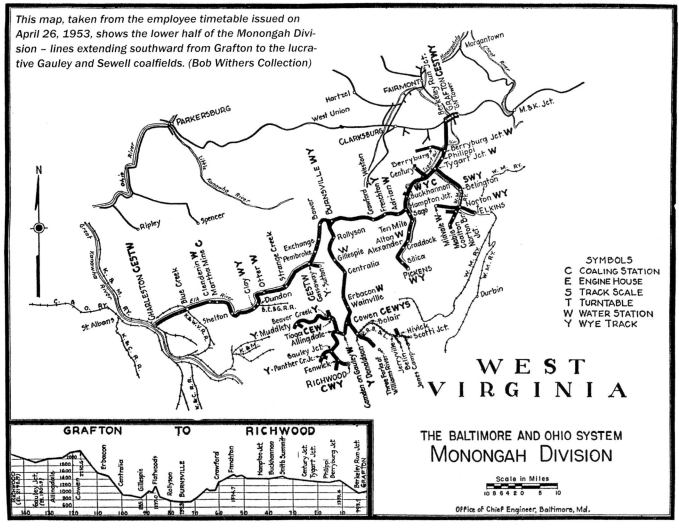

This map, taken from the employee timetable issued on April 26, 1953, shows the lower half of the Monongah Division – lines extending southward from Grafton to the lucrative Gauley and Sewell coalfields. (Bob Withers Collection)

SYMBOLS
C COALING STATION
E ENGINE HOUSE
S TRACK SCALE
T TURNTABLE
W WATER STATION
Y WYE TRACK

WEST VIRGINIA

THE BALTIMORE AND OHIO SYSTEM
MONONGAH DIVISION

Scale in Miles
10 8 6 4 2 0   5   10

Office of Chief Engineer, Baltimore, Md.

GRAFTON TO RICHWOOD

Opposite: This passenger run crossing the Tygart Valley River Bridge in Grafton is unidentified, but it probably is Train 136 from Charleston, the state capital, which was due in Grafton in the early afternoon. (B&O RR Historical Society, TLC Collection)

This tiny train order office at Berryburg Jct., seen at 10:40 a.m. on July 13, 1961, dates from the 1930s. The company had to relocate several miles of the old Grafton & Belington predecessor line because of the construction of the Tygart Valley Dam. (Bob Withers photo)

Class Q-3 MacArthur 4531 assembles loads of coal on the Berryburg Branch in August 1954. (W.E. Hopkins photo, Bob Withers Collection)

Class E-60 Consolidation 3130 is assigned to a Berryburg Branch mine run in August 1954. The tiny Alco-built 2-8-0 is far from home – it began life as Buffalo & Susquehanna No. 156 in October 1907 and her date with the torch is just days away. (W.E. Hopkins photo, Bob Withers Collection)

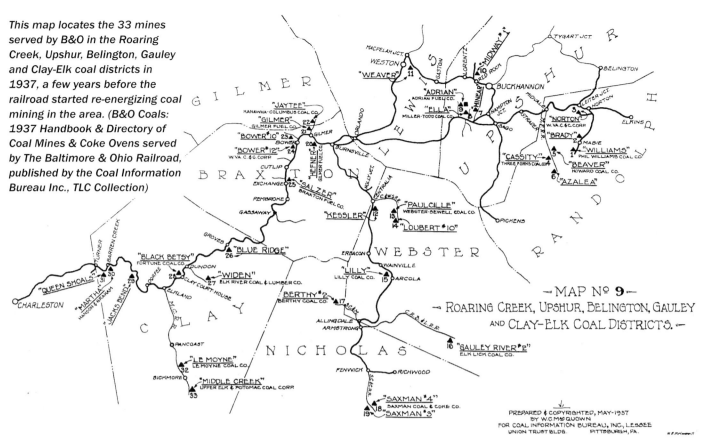

This map locates the 33 mines served by B&O in the Roaring Creek, Upshur, Belington, Gauley and Clay-Elk coal districts in 1937, a few years before the railroad started re-energizing coal mining in the area. (B&O Coals: 1937 Handbook & Directory of Coal Mines & Coke Ovens served by The Baltimore & Ohio Railroad, published by the Coal Information Bureau Inc., TLC Collection)

GP9 6521 leads one of several daily drags past the Spanish-styled station at Philippi in July 1964. At the time, Cowen is pumping out something like 2,500 carloads of coal each week toward the assembly yard at Grafton. (James B. Kelley photo, Bob Withers Collection)

B. & O. Station, BELINGTON, W. Va.

A few patrons await the arrival of a train at the Belington station in this early post card view. The old G&B line continues toward Elkins – and so does the Western Maryland from this point. [TLC Collection)

A B&O special operated for an engineering party stops at Norton on the line toward Elkins on Dec. 9, 1940. The four-wheel caboose, of Coal & Coke heritage, is C1703. The line back to Belington swings toward the left. (TLC Collection)

Class B-8 Ten-Wheeler 1373 pauses with Weston-Pickens local No. 101 at Buckhannon on a fine autumn day in October 1938. Baldwin built the tiny locomotive in May 1893; it will operate for nine more years before going to scrap. (Jay Williams Collection)

Even after the Grafton-Cowen line was rebuilt, the USRA light Q-3 class MacArthurs in the 4500 series were the heaviest locomotives permitted over most of the route. Even so, there was plenty of work for them to do. Here, the photographer captures Class Q-3 4592 hauling a wayfreight near Buckhannon on July 1, 1956. (Jim Shaughnessy photo, Bob Withers Collection)

Class Q-3 4588 rests between runs at Buckhannon in August 1954. In those days, empties left Grafton behind a single Q-3. Another Q-3 was added in Buckhannon for the remainder of the run to Cowen. Returning from there with tonnage, the two Mikes got an assist from two more Mikes from Gillespie that had run light from Buckhannon. Upon arrival in Buckhannon, three Mikes were cut off and a single engine took the loads into Grafton. (W.E. Hopkins photo, Bob Withers Collection)

Class Q-3 MacArthur 4587 and two other light 2-8-2's rest between runs at Buckhannon's outdoor servicing facility on July 1, 1956. (Jim Shaughnessy photo, Bob Withers Collection)

Buckhannon-Pickens mixed Train 453 carried no mail in the mid-1940s but maybe a few passengers and a package or two of express in addition to its freight cars. It hung on longer than many of B&O's mixed trains, being needed to haul schoolchildren living in the remote hills and hollows to and from classes in Buckhannon. Class E-60 Consolidation 3130 rumbles toward Pickens on this particular afternoon. (Bob Withers Collection)

The photo is undated, but at least a few people are hanging around the Pickens station waiting the arrival of mixed train 453. (Bob Withers Collection)

A long line of railroaders pose with Q-3 MacArthur 334 (4535 until the 1956 renumbering) at Burnsville Junction in the summer of 1957. The Mike, headed toward Grafton, is sitting on the line from Richwood. The Elk Subdivision to Charleston can be seen diverging to the left. We do not know why so many workers are present – maybe the occasion is someone's retirement. (Bob Withers Collection)

Track forces with a work train dump slag on a fill at one end of the Camp Run washout near Centralia on July 20, 1949. Class E-27ca Consolidation 2833 is coupled to caboose C2309, which started life as a boxcar but was converted by the Mount Clare Shops in late 1942 to relieve a chronic World War II caboose shortage. (TLC Collection)

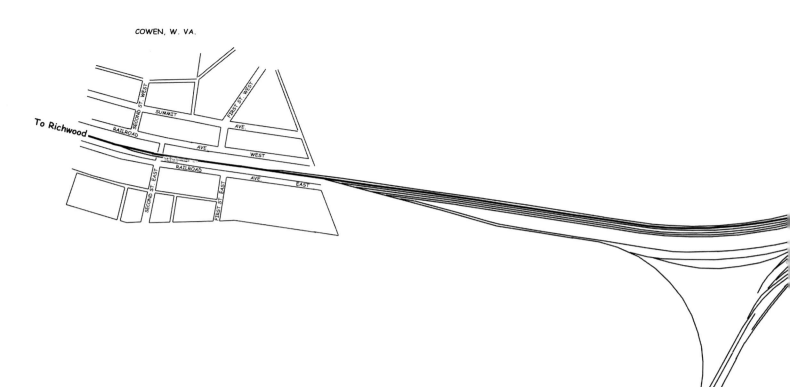

To Richwood

WN Tower, seen here at 6:55 a.m. on July 21, 1964, is where crews leaving Cowen for Grafton receive their train orders, messages, and clearance cards. The building's size belies its around-the-clock workload. (Jan G. Weiford photo, Bob Withers Collection)

To Grafton

The Cowen Yard and engine terminal was built during World War II at the point where the Williams River Branch joined the line to Richwood. By 1950, the installation included a 262-car receiving yard, a 228-car dispatching yard, a brick engine house, a cinder conveyor, a track scale, sand and water supplies, and dormitory, mess hall and sanitary facilities for train crews. The company's decision to develop the Gauley-Sewell Field came at an opportune time – Large-scale operators from the New River territory to the south along the Chesapeake & Ohio Railway were exhausting their reserves and looking for new opportunities. Several of them relocated to the Gauley-Sewell Field. (B&O RR Historical Society archive)

B&O mine runs accessed Bolair Mines 1 and 2 at Bolair, owned by Kessler Coal Co. of Cowen, via trackage rights on the Cherry River Boom & Lumber Co. from Donaldson on the Williams River Branch. In 1949, they contributed 10 daily carloads of run-of-mine coal to B&O's bottom line. (B&O RR Historical Society archive)

Gauley No. 2 Mine at Jerryville, owned by the Elk Lick Coal Co., also was located on the CRB&L Co. Opened in 1933, it produced an output of 224,246 tons in 1948. (B&O RR Historical Society archive)

The photographer captured a photo of this compact combination station at Allingdale, where B&O's Richwood line connected with the leased Strouds Creek & Muddlety short line, at 9:35 a.m. on July 21, 1964. Once B&O leased the 12.4-mile SC&M, it was extended 11 miles by purchasing and rehabilitating the Birch Valley Lumber Co.'s track. (Jan G. Weiford photo, Bob Withers Collection)

Donegan Coal & Coke Co.'s Donegan mine was located on the Saxman Branch, which diverged from the Richwood line at Fenwick. Opened in 1943, the mine's 1948 output was 141,804 tons. B&O rehabilitated the branch, which it purchased from the Ely Thomas Lumber Co. (B&O RR Historical Society archive)

We have returned to Burnsville Junction, as it were, and are headed down the Elk Subdivision toward Charleston. This is the impressive station at Bower, 15 miles north of Gassaway, ca. 1920. The Coal & Coke Railway managed an impressive freight, coal and passenger business until the day it was taken into the B&O system in 1918. (TLC Collection)

Even more impressive than the station at Bower is the stone-and-brick passenger depot in Gassaway, seen here at 3:10 p.m. on July 12, 1961. Gassaway boasted a fair-sized yard and locomotive servicing facility, and the station's attic was a treasure trove of ancient employee timetables and train registers well into the 1960s. (Bob Withers photo)

Class E-8₆₀ Consolidation 1212 looks like it is in storage in Gassaway in June 1940. Baldwin built the tiny engine in March 1892 and it was scrapped in July 1948. (Harold K. Vollrath photo, Bob Withers Collection)

The combination station at Falling Rock, 17 miles north of Charleston, is seen at 5 p.m. on Saturday, June 1, 1963. The building was a two-story frame affair – a relative rarity on B&O. (John P. Killoran photo, Bob Withers Collection)

Now we proceed westward from Grafton toward Parkersburg, diverging only briefly to run up the Astor and Bear Mountain branches to inspect Mountain Fuel Co.'s Glen Cambria tipple. In 1937, this mine turned out 36 daily carloads. (B&O Coals: 1937 Handbook & Directory of Coal Mines & Coke Ovens served by The Baltimore & Ohio Railroad, published by the Coal Information Bureau Inc., TLC Collection)

Business was impressive enough – at least for a while – to warrant a brick combination station at Flemington, seen here on Nov. 27, 1939. (TLC Collection)

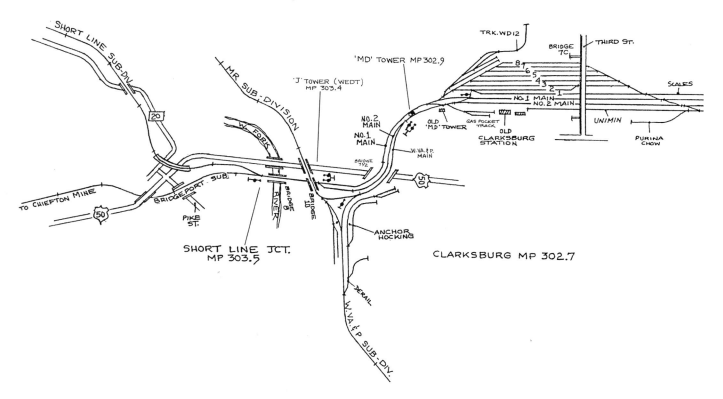

A mine run powered by GP9's 6479, 6485, and 6499, brings 76 loads and caboose C2000 from the Wilsonburg area into Clarksburg at 3:37 p.m. on Wednesday, July 3, 1963. The photographer is shooting from MD Tower just west of the station and yard office. At 4:23, the engines and their caboose will go by MD in the opposite direction, headed for West Fork Shops. (Bob Withers photo)

James R. "Monty" Montgomery smiles for a photographer in the cab of GP9 6521 at Clarksburg's West Fork Shops in 1957. This is Monty's first road trip as engineer of a regular turn on a diesel. He has bid on – and been assigned to – Trains 100 and 99 between Clarksburg and Benwood via the Short Line, a train he fired on countless occasions in steam days. At the time, timetable direction on the Short Line was the reverse of geographical direction because many pairs of Short Line trains, including this one, also operated on the Wheeling Division between Brooklyn Junction and Benwood. (Bob Withers Collection)

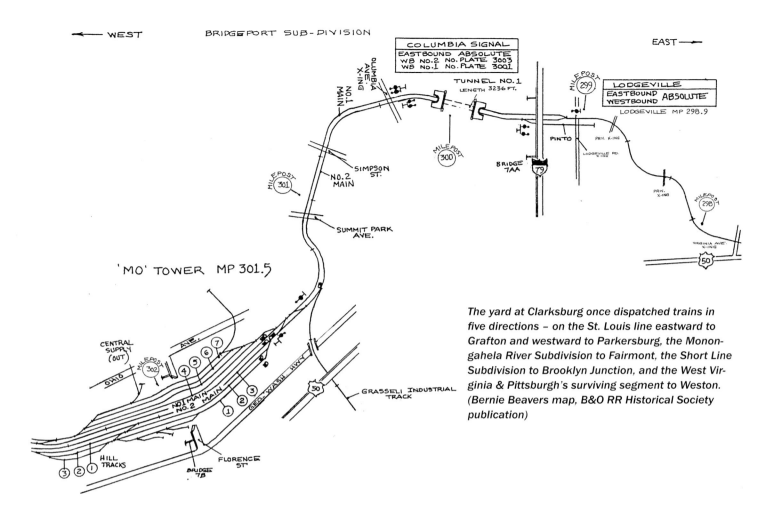

COLUMBIA SIGNAL
EASTBOUND ABSOLUTE
WB No.2 No. PLATE 3003
WB No.1 No. PLATE 3001

TUNNEL No. 1
LENGTH 3236 FT.

LODGEVILLE
EASTBOUND
WESTBOUND ABSOLUTE
LODGEVILLE MP 298.9

COLUMBIA AVE. X-ING

No.1 MAIN

MILEPOST 299

SIMPSON ST.

MILEPOST 300

No.2 MAIN

MILEPOST 301

PINTO

PRIV. X-ING
LODGEVILLE RD. X-ING

BRIDGE 7AA

79

PRIV. X-ING

MILEPOST 298

SUMMIT PARK AVE.

VIRGINIA AVE. X-ING

50

'MO' TOWER MP 301.5

CENTRAL SUPPLY (OUT)

OHIO

AVE.

7

MILEPOST 302

5 6

4

3

2

1

No.1 MAIN
No.2 MAIN

GEO. WASH. HWY

50

GRASSELI INDUSTRIAL TRACK

HILL TRACKS

3 2 1

BRIDGE 7B

FLORENCE ST

The yard at Clarksburg once dispatched trains in five directions – on the St. Louis line eastward to Grafton and westward to Parkersburg, the Monongahela River Subdivision to Fairmont, the Short Line Subdivision to Brooklyn Junction, and the West Virginia & Pittsburgh's surviving segment to Weston. (Bernie Beavers map, B&O RR Historical Society publication)

Class E-32 Consolidation 1738 sits at Weston between runs on Aug. 16, 1937. This ex-Coal & Coke locomotive – built by Baldwin in April 1904 as C&C No. 12, was renumbered 41 under C&C management and became 1738 when B&O took over C&C in 1918. The engine may have had a long entry in the rosters, but it never strayed too awfully far from home. Its date with the torch came in July 1938, not quite a year after this photo was made. (C.L. Collum photo, John A. Rehor Collection)

The crew of the Dola mine run on the Short Line Subdivision poses with Q-3 MacArthur 4588 in the mid-1950s. Crew members include engineer Russ Glover, left; engineer Charles B. Hughes, third from left; and brakeman Ira Starkey, second from right. The presence of two engineers is explained by the fact that B&O's mine runs usually used two locomotives – one at the head end of the train and one at the rear. The head-end locomotive pulled loads from mines with trailing-point switches and the rear-end engine pulled them away from tipples accessed by facing-point switches. (Bob Withers Collection)

We're back now on the Clarksburg-Parkersburg main line, looking at the station at Wolf Summit ca. 1920. Note the four-wheel caboose nearly rolling out of the picture at right. (B&O RR Historical Society archive, Bob Withers Collection)

The brick station at Salem hosts several passengers while they await their train ca. 1920. Salem remained a regular stop until Amtrak Day on May 1, 1971. (B&O RR Historical Society archive, Bob Withers Collection)

The frame combination station at Smithburg is seen on Aug. 27, 1977, long after passenger trains stopped stopping there. At last account, the restored building still exists – although tracks are nowhere to be seen. (C.J. Bocklage Jr. photo, TLC Collection)

The brick combination station at Pennsboro is seen on Aug. 27, 1977. Like Salem, it remained a regular stop until the advent of Amtrak. (C.J. Bocklage Jr. photo, TLC Collection)

This is Cairo, looking west. The station, in the distance at right, did not welcome passengers in its later years but lasted until a derailment in the 1960s took it out. (B&O RR Historical Society archive, Bob Withers Collection)

We are entering Parkersburg, but we pause for a look at the massive coaling station. It's Sept. 4, 1932, and it looks like a workman is installing a number plate on the smokebox of Class E-33 Consolidation 2941 as a larger locomotive awaits attention in the distance. Baldwin built the 2-8-0 for the Coal & Coke in May 1906 and it was retired in December 1944. (TLC Collection)

Class B-8b Ten-Wheeler 1383 slumbers at the Parkersburg servicing facility in the 1940s. Of the 58 B-8's built by B&O and Baldwin in 1891-93, it was the only locomotive of its class to be rebuilt so extensively that it became known locally as "the Queen of the Fleet." Originally built for high-speed passenger service, the tiny locomotives accepted any and all assignments during their golden years. Baldwin turned out the 1383 in May 1893 and it was sold for scrap in June 1951. [Harold Wetherall, Bob Withers Collection)

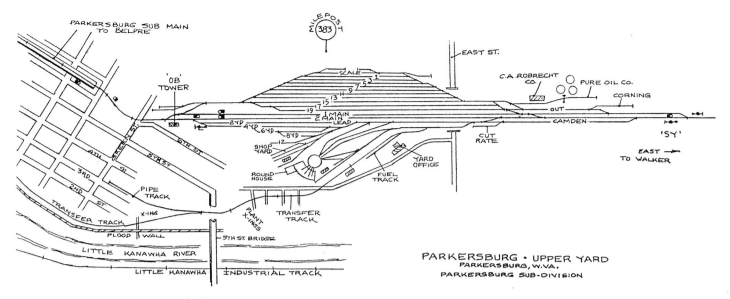

Parkersburg's High Yard ran east-to-west along the St. Louis line. OB Tower shows up on this map from the 1980s, but the Sixth Street Station, which stood in the curve west of Green Street, was torn down in 1973 to make room for a bank parking lot. Note the transfer track leading to the Low Yard, which for years was part of the Wheeling Division. Today, neither the east-west main line nor its once-luxurious passenger trains exist, but the High Yard is still used to access the Marietta Sub across the Ohio River and for car storage. (Bernie Beavers map, B&O RR Historical Society publication)

Class D-30 0-6-0 switcher 357 handles a cut of passenger cars next to Parkersburg's OB Tower and across Green Street from the Sixth Street Station ca. 1934. Baldwin built the engine to a USRA design in May 1919. It was renumbered to 1157 to 1950 and scrapped in December 1953. (Jay Williams Collection)

*This photo looks west from OB Tower toward Parkersburg's Sixth Street Station ca. 1935.
The main lines come together just before crossing the Ohio River Bridge to the right, and
storage tracks hold set-out cars to the left. (TLC Collection)*

*Passengers at the Sixth Street Station seem more inter-
ested in the photographer than the train for which they
are waiting in 1897. The station was built when the B&O-
backed Northwestern Virginia railroad reached Parkersburg
in 1857. The Ohio River Bridge, behind the camera, was
opened in 1871. (Artcraft Studio, Bob Withers Collection)*

A motor car and trailer comprise Train 44 from Portsmouth, Ohio, as it crosses the Ohio River Bridge into Parkersburg on Saturday, July 13, 1946. The tracks below the bridge are part of the Wheeling Division's Ohio River Subdivision, and it looks like the old Ohio River Railroad freight house is about to come down. (John F. Humiston photo, TLC Collection)

Class P-1d Pacific 5068 takes a nine-car troop train out of Grafton on the afternoon of Wednesday, May 20, 1953. Aboard its eight heavyweight sleepers and midtrain Army kitchen car are 202 Army draftees en route from Fort George G. Meade, Md., to 16 weeks of Infantry basic training at Camp Breckenridge, Ky. The signing of an armistice ending the Korean War barely two months later also will signal the end, for all practical purposes, of the troop train era. This excellent scene also shows a significant portion of the Grafton yard – the impressive station and towering old Willard Hotel at left and the large concrete coaling station that dominated the western end of the yard at left. In 1953, Grafton is a key operational point for main line trains and a key assembly point for coal from several branch lines from the north, northwest and south. (Philip R. Hastings photo, Bob Withers Collection)

4: The Wheeling Division

At the midpoint of the 20th century, the Baltimore & Ohio's Wheeling Division stretched from Cleveland to Kenova, W.Va., appearing on maps to be sort of a north-south spinal cord that stitched the rest of the 13-state system together.

The division's West Virginia portion started life as the 208-mile Ohio River Railroad, which began building southward from Benwood, four miles south of Wheeling, in 1883. The track reached Parkersburg in 1884, Point Pleasant in late 1886 and Guyandotte in 1888. Trains rumbled on for three more miles into Huntington on the Chesapeake & Ohio Railway until 1892, when the Ohio River Railroad leased the locally backed Huntington & Big Sandy, which gave it nearly 12 more miles of line into Kenova. B&O acquired control of the road in 1901 — which included the 32.7-mile Ravenswood, Spencer & Glenville and the 12.3-mile Ripley & Mill Creek Valley branches —by buying the company's stock; the property was deeded to B&O in 1912.

The branches' mixed and freight trains hauled basically livestock and agricultural supplies. But the main line's first traffic was lucrative crude oil, which was logical since the railroad had been constructed almost as an accessory of Standard Oil. In time a flourishing passenger trade developed, but freight tonnage remained fairly light until several industrial plants went up on the wide bottomlands of the Ohio after World War II. That development held at bay a couple of discussions about the possible abandonment of parts of the line until low-sulfur coal from the southern part of the state started rolling toward power plants up north in 1994. The closing of the Baltimore-St. Louis main line's midsection in 1985

Kenova-to-Pittsburgh Train 72, pulled by Class P-1d Pacific 5092, crosses the graceful stone arch viaduct in the Tunnel Green section of Wheeling on a pleasant evening in May 1950. The spot is east of the Wheeling passenger station but still short of the Pittsburgh Division marker. (J.J. Young Jr. photo, Bob Withers Collection)

and the resulting redirection of much of its freight traffic to the Ohio River line didn't hurt, either.

Of course, the branches were long gone by then. The R&MCV was closed in 1963; RS&G traffic was embargoed in 1968 and the line, with its 69 timber trestles, was ripped up by 1970.

The Wheeling Division extended in a north-south orientation all the way from Lake Erie to the Tri-State Area where West Virginia, Ohio and Kentucky meet. Of course, for the purposes of this book, we will examine only that part of the division that was in West Virginia. (Bob Withers Collection)

SYMBOLS
C — COALING STATION
E — ENGINE HOUSE
S — TRACK SCALE
T — TURNTABLE
W — WATER STATION
Y — WYE TRACK

THE BALTIMORE AND OHIO SYSTEM
WHEELING DIVISION
Scale in Miles

B. & O. DEPOT SHOWING
TRAIN-SHEDS AND VIADUCT
WHEELING, W.VA.

A mighty Class EM-1 2-8-8-4 articulated locomotive crosses the Ohio River bridge at Benwood Junction in March 1954 with another trainload of coal for the Lake Erie port of Lorain, Ohio. The EM-1's, numbered in the 7600-7629 series (650-679 after Nov. 1, 1956) had been bumped from the mountainous lines of the Cumberland and Monongah divisions by the incessant onslaught of diesels. (J.J. Young Jr. photo, Bob Withers Collection)

After diesels dispatched the EM-1's from B&O's main lines, Benwood became one of their home terminals. Here, engines 650, 676, and another unidentified member of the class in the distance between them are serviced for their next runs in August 1957. Even with all their power and their young ages, they're living on borrowed time. (J.J. Young Jr. photo, Bob Withers Collection)

The biblical Book of Revelation says the number of the beast is 666. This photo shows that there is a mechanical as well as spiritual application to that truth. Class EM-1 2-8-8-4 No. 666 is resting between runs in the Benwood Junction roundhouse on Sept. 25, 1957. (Bruce D. Fales photo, Jay Williams Collection)

Operator Francis South hands up track assignment instructions to the engineer of incoming Train 98, a Parkersburg-Benwood freight train, at SW Tower in McMechen, just south of Benwood, during a January 1954 snowfall. The 4473 is a Class Q-4b MacArthur – in B&O terminology. (J.J. Young Jr. photo, Bob Withers Collection)

Operator Paul Maxwell repeats a train order for an oncoming train at SW Tower on Saturday, Feb. 23, 1957. (J.J. Young Jr. photo, Bob Withers Collection)

This map shows that at one time, coal mines could be found even along the Wheeling Division in northern West Virginia. (B&O Coals: 1937 Handbook & Directory of Coal Mines & Coke Ovens served by The Baltimore & Ohio Railroad, published by the Coal Information Bureau Inc., TLC Collection)

The Chessie System era has dawned as an eastbound diesel-powered Train 204 rumbles past the combination station at Clarington, 26.8 miles below Wheeling, in the early 1970s. The unincorporated community on the West Virginia side of the Ohio River is called Kent; the depot is named for the town on the Ohio side – evidence that a ferry boat once connected the two. (Chessie System photo, Bob Withers Collection)

Class P-6a Pacific 5231 departs Moundsville with Train 73. We know the photo was made between Sept. 1, 1955, and Jan. 31, 1957, since the train consists of merely an express car and coach. Its baggage/mail RPO car made its last trip on Aug. 31, 1955. The station, incidentally, was disguised as "Glory" for the James Stewart movie "Fool's Parade" several years later. (J.J. Young Jr. photo, Bob Withers Collection)

The New Martinsville station was a popular gathering spot in the early years of the 20th century, when most travel between communities was by rail. These folks are all dressed up in anticipation of a Parkersburg train from the South, a Wheeling train from the North, or a Clarksburg train from the East. (AAA Homes 2003 calendar, Bob Withers Collection)

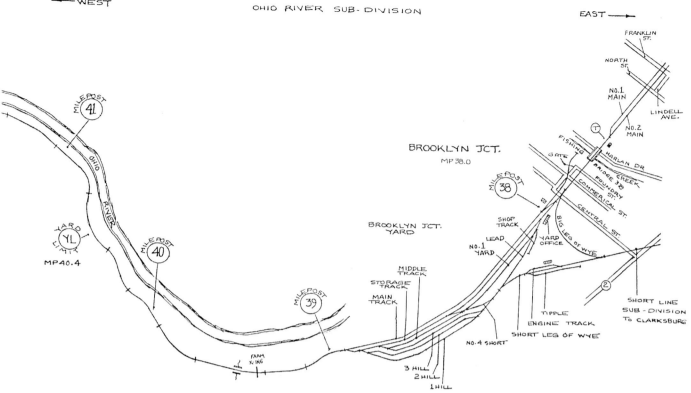

This map shows the yard at Brooklyn Junction, just south of New Martinsville. Until 1961, the Ohio River Subdivision was part of the Wheeling Division and only the Short Line Sub belonged to the Monongah Division. By the time this map was made, the new Martinsville station was gone, but it stood just west of the North Street crossing on the north side of the double-track Ohio River Sub main line. (Bernie Beavers map, B&O RR Historical Society publication)

Agent/Operator Gideon "Gid" Brown, a Mason County native, is more than 130 miles from home as he poses on the station platform in the tiny Pleasants County community of Raven Rock, population fewer than 100, in 1902. The helpful station sign not only informs passengers where they are, but also that they are 59.5 miles from Wheeling and 163.4 miles from Kenova. Brown's sons Wallace and Garland also became agent/operators, working at various Ohio River line stations including Apple Grove and Huntington. (Garland T. Brown, Bob Withers Collection)

All seems quiet at the combination station in St. Marys on Dec. 23, 1954. Well, after all, it's only two days until Christmas. (Bob Withers Collection)

Class P-5a Pacific 5213 brings Train 73 into Parkersburg's Ann Street Station in the early 1950s. The locomotive, which hauled the very first all-Pullman Capitol Limited out of Baltimore's Mount Royal Station on May 13, 1923, was sold for scrap in December 1953. (Artcraft Studio photo, Bob Withers Collection)

Conductor Clyde Barker (left) and trainman Bill Downs pose beside Train 73 at Ann Street Station in August 1948. (O.V. Nelson photo, Bob Withers Collection)

Opposite: It's the fall of 1934, and we're standing on the elevated platform of Parkersburg's Ann Street Station looking at Class P-3 Pacific 5100 heading around the transfer track to the High Yard. The locomotive has just arrived at Ann Street with 12 Pennsylvania Railroad coaches loaded with students from Weirton High School. The students have disembarked and the train has backed off the elevated platform to head uptown for servicing. While Weirton football team members battle it out with their Big Red opponents at Parkersburg High, the engine will receive new helpings of coal and water and the train will be taken to Belpre, Ohio, to be turned on a wye. (Stephen P. Davidson photo, Bob Withers Collection)

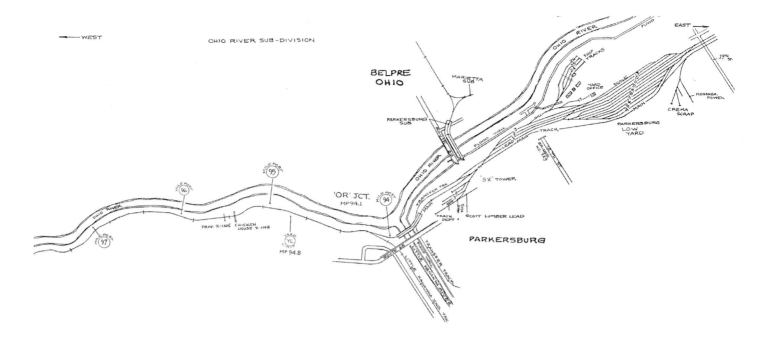

With Class P-6a Pacific 5231's headlight burning brightly, Train 73 arrives at Ann Street for the last time on Jan. 31, 1957. In addition to the express car and regular coach, the train carries a tourist sleeper – courtesy of Wheeling Division Superintendent John J. Sell – to accommodate all the deadheads and spouses who want to take the last ride. (Artcraft Studio, Bob Withers Collection)

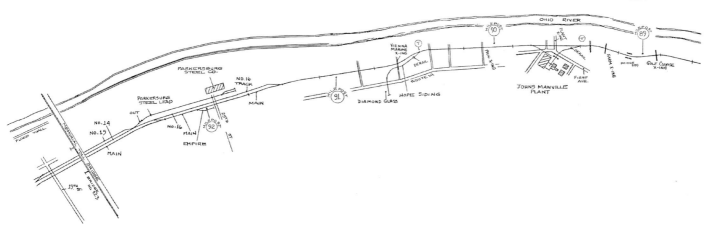

Parkersburg's Low Yard was built by B&O predecessor Ohio River Railroad – and expanded several times by B&O – along the Ohio River on a north-south orientation. This map was produced in the late 1980s and thus does not show the Ann Street Station, which was torn down in 1959. But the reader can see on the map where it once stood – at the north end of the Little Kanawha River bridge between the main line and the transfer track to the east-west High Yard. The transfer on the map, which ran along the western and southern walls of Ann Street, was built in 1956 to replace the old transfer seen in the photo below, which ran along the north wall and into 2nd Street. (Bernie Beavers map, B&O RR Historical Society publication)

Class B-18e Ten-Wheeler 2061 is backing up the transfer track past Parkersburg's Ann Street Station in June 1953. The engine has just delivered mixed Train 82 to the Low Yard and is backing up 2nd Street – notice the flagman on the tender's footboard – toward the roundhouse in the High Yard for servicing. By the end of the year, the 2061 and its five surviving mates will be out of service. (TLC Collection)

Work Extra 4206, the DuPont District Run, crosses the Little Kanawha River bridge in Parkersburg en route to several plants six miles down the river on Jan. 15, 1982. Both the Little Kanawha and the Ohio rivers are completely frozen over. The photographer was taking a picture of his own turn – at least it was his own turn until fireman Charlie Sayre bumped him a few days before. (David Corbitt photo, H.L. "Bud" Gray Collection)

The original station at Belleville, shown here, was destroyed by the 1913 Ohio River flood, but was replaced with a "modern" building on the high side of the track. Agents stayed on the job there until the mid-1950s. (Bob Withers Collection)

Class P-5a Pacific 5229 is charging into RS&G Junction, just below Ravenswood, with a four-car Train 73 on Tuesday, Oct. 23, 1951. The fireman either doesn't know how to ensure a clean stack or is fulfilling a request by the photographer. (Richard J. Cook photo, Bob Withers Collection)

Head brakeman/baggagemaster Glen Yost, having helped about a dozen members of the Collis P. Huntington chapter of the National Railway Historical Society and Assistant Trainmaster F.L. McGaha onto combine 1399, takes a break in the baggage compartment as mixed Train 457 heads out the 32.7-mile RS&G Branch for Spencer on Saturday, April 16, 1960. Another chapter member – 15-year-old "Bobby" Withers – is riding in Baldwin 1,000-horsepower switcher 9248 with engineer Johnny Lightner and fireman Dave Brown. (John P. Killoran photo, Bob Withers Collection)

Flagman "Curly" Clark, left, and head brakeman/baggagemaster Charles Shank oblige the photographer with a pose as they load a farmer's can of cream into combine 1397 aboard mixed Train 458 at Sandyville on Oct. 23, 1951. (Richard J. Cook photo, Bob Withers Collection)

Class B-18d Ten-Wheeler 2026 loafs down a steep 2.96 percent grade as it crosses a timber trestle just past Sandy Summit with mixed Train 458 on Oct. 23, 1951. The 32.7-mile Ravenswood-Spencer branch had 69 timber trestles of varying heights and lengths – more than two per mile. (Richard J. Cook photo, Bob Withers Collection)

Class B-8a Ten-Wheeler 1365, at the head end of Spencer-to-Ravenswood mixed Train 68 at Reedy in about 1936, has taken water and is waiting for a helper engine to quench its thirst, too. (Dr. Howard N. Blackburn photo, Jay Williams Collection)

Head brakeman/baggage-master Charles Shank carries some waybills back to mixed Train 458 engine 2026 at Reedy on Oct. 23, 1951. (Richard J. Cook photo, Bob Withers Collection)

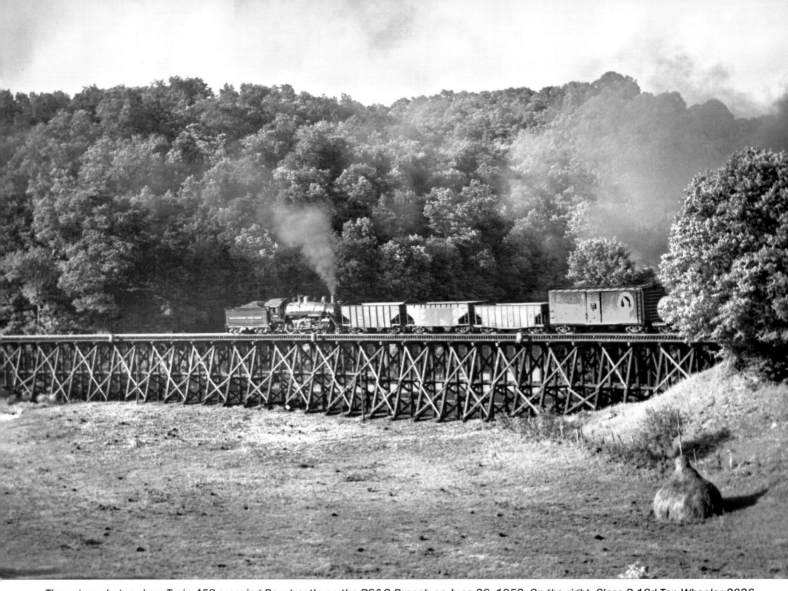

These two photos show Train 458 crossing Barr trestle on the RS&G Branch on June 26, 1952. On the right, Class B-18d Ten-Wheeler 2026 leads the train. On the left, Class B-18c Ten-Wheeler 2020 shoves the same train across Barr trestle. An examination of these two photos reveals that Train 458 is carrying the combine and nine cars on this trip. RS&G trains more often than not operated with pushers in the

Hopefully, this is as close to a cornfield meet as any two trains ever will have. Passenger Train 72, at left, powered by Class P-6a Pacific 5244, has made its station stop at Millwood and is proceeding eastward on the Ohio River Subdivision at 4:38 p.m. on Sept. 12, 1956, while Train 73 engine 5241 waits in the passing siding. (W.J.B. Gwinn photo, Bob Withers Collection)

steam days. Motive power was restricted to the smaller engines because of light rail, spindly trestles and sharp curves, yet they faced dozens of steep grades – several of them more than 3 percent. (Richard J. Cook photos, Bob Withers Collection)

With 72 by, Train 73 will back out of the siding and ease down to the Millwood station for its scheduled stop since the 69-car passing siding has freight cars standing on its western end. No. 72 is an hour late, and No. 73 is more than an hour late – unless the photographer/passenger's notes refer to daylight savings time. (W.J.B. Gwinn photo, Bob Withers Collection)

The station at Millwood is seen here just after it closed on June 30, 1962. The old building met its demise without ever having electric power or a Bell telephone. (John P. Killoran photo, Bob Withers Collection)

Class B-18c Ten-Wheeler 2020 and a single coach are ready to leave Ripley as mixed Train 962 on Wednesday, Oct. 24, 1951. The locomotive really earns its keep on this run. it departs Parkersburg about daylight on mixed Train 81, puts its train in the siding at Millwood and runs out to Ripley and back on the 12.3-mile Ripley & Mill Creek Valley Branch, then resumes its trek at the head end of Train 81 to Kenova. A long day, indeed. (Richard J. Cook photo, Bob Withers Collection)

Alas, Ten-Wheelers on the branches in Jackson and Roane counties were not to last. Here, Baldwin Class VO1000 switcher 428 has brought Train 961 into Ripley on Dec. 17, 1953 – the first diesel into Ripley. Posing for the occasion are, from left, engineer Vic Davis, fireman James R. "Monty" Montgomery, Eastern Region Supervisor of Locomotive Operations D.J. Ferrell, conductor Tommy Thompson, and retired Ripley agent C.E. Flesher. By changing the overnight terminal of Nos. 457-458 from Spencer to Ravenswood, altering the schedules of Nos. 961-962 to the late afternoon and divorcing them from Train 81, and changing the home terminal of a district run from Point Pleasant to Ravenswood, Jack Ferrell managed to replace – and retire – six Ten Wheelers and one Consolidation with a single 1,000-horsepower yard engine. (Don Flesher photo, Bob Withers Collection)

The Mason City depot stood roughly halfway between Parkersburg and Kenova. Sharp eyes may see a little boy loafing next to the baggage truck and another seated in the shade of the waiting room. In later years the station lost its waiting room and is totally gone today, but passersby still can see the old brick platform – including the cutout where the bay window once stood. (C.R. Davidson, Bob Withers Collection)

Union Depot, B. & O. K. & M., Pt. Pleasant, W. Va.

Point Pleasant yard was turned inside out in 1909 when the New York Central relocated its tracks from under the B&O line to the hillside above it. At NYC's expense, the B&O passenger station that dated from the 1890s was expanded and became a union depot. NYC passengers reached the waiting room via the sheltered concrete steps at left. (Mid-America Paper Collectibles, Bob Withers Collection)

With conductor James Duvall and engineer John W. Worley in charge, Class B-8a Ten-Wheeler 1377 takes Train 72 across the new Kanawha River bridge into Point Pleasant at 2:40 p.m. on Thursday, April 17, 1947. Soon, the tiny engine will give way to heavier Ten-Wheelers, MacArthurs, and Pacifics now that the West End's weakest link is gone. The 1887 structure the span replaced is in the foreground; its piers still stand. (The [Huntington] Herald-Advertiser of April 20, 1947, Bob Withers Collection)

The expansive union depot at Point Pleasant had outlived its usefulness by 1960, so B&O purchased the old NYC freight house – which was positioned alongside the B&O/NYC transfer out of sight to the left – to be its "new" station. Here, on Thursday, May 26, engineer Harry E. Nixon carefully eases the replacement structure – mounted on two flatcars – toward its location facing the B&O main line. (Bob Withers Collection)

Guyandotte became a part of Huntington in 1911, but for years it was an independent town. In fact, it served as predecessor Ohio River Railroad's western terminus from 1888 to 1892. The combination depot was torn down in 1934. (Helen Diddle, Bob Withers Collection)

In the summer of 1960, the photographer has discovered a fantastic perch to capture the entire consist of thrice-weekly mixed Train 81 as it enters Huntington. Behind the GP9 are combine 1449, a peddler car, six loads of gasoline picked up at the Gulf Oil Corp. bulk depot just east of town, four other cars added farther up the river, and caboose C2261. (John P. Killoran photo, Bob Withers Collection)

B&O LOCAL TRAIN SERVICE
Parkersburg and Huntington
Train 81—Monday, Wednesday and Friday only.
Train 82—Tuesday, Thursday and Saturday only.

81 Mixed	Miles	Westward (Read Down)	Eastward (Read Up) (Opposite Ohio Towns)	82 Mixed
AM				PM
6.55	0.0	Lv *Parkersburg (Fifth St. Sta.)...Belpre, O. Ar		1.15
f7.08	2.5	Blennerhassett		f1.01
f7.17	6.1	Washington		12 f52
f7.20	7.3	Tallmans		12 f49
f7.24	9.0	Meldahls		12 f45
f7.29	11.4	New England		12 f40
f7.34	13.6	Harris Ferry...Hockingport, O.		12 f35
f7.39	15.8	Lee Creek		12 f30
f7.42	16.9	Humphrey		12 f27
7.44	17.8	Belleville...Reedsville, O.		12 f25
f7.48	19.8	Pond Creek		12 f21
f7.51	21.0	Lone Cedar		12 f18
f7.54	22.3	Neptune		12 f15
f7.58	24.0	Murrayville...Long Bottom, O.		12 f11
f8.04	27.4	Polk		12 f05
f8.08	30.2	Morgan		12 f01
f8.11	30.9	Portland...Portland, O.		11 f57
f8.13	33.1	Sherman		11 f55
8.20	34.6	Ravenswood		11.45
8.30	38.5	Pleasant View		11 f35
f8.34	40.3	Hills Crossing		11 f31
f8.38	41.7	Ravenswood Works		11 f27
f8.44	44.4	Estar		11 f21
8.47	45.6	Millwood...Apple Grove, O.		11.18
8.57	50.6	Letart...Letart Falls, O.		11.08
f9.03	53.3	Longdale		11 f04
f9.09	56.1	Graham...Racine, O.		10 f43
9.25	59.4	New Haven...Syracuse, O.		10.36
9.29	61.1	Hartford...Minersville, O.		10.32
9.35	63.9	Mason City...Pomeroy, O.		10.26
f9.39	65.6	Clifton...Middleport, O.		10 f22
f9.43	67.4	West Columbia...Hobson, O.		10 f18
f9.45	68.2	Hallwood		10 f16
f9.49	69.8	Lakin		10 f12
f9.59	74.3	York		10 f02
10.22	78.9	Point Pleasant...Kanauga, O.		9.24
10 f40	80.1	Henderson		f9.20
10.50	84.5	Gallipolis...Gallipolis, O.		9.11
f1 f02	90.4	Ben Lomond		f8.58
11 f06	91.7	Hogsett...Eureka, O.		f8.55
11 f11	93.9	Apple Grove...Bladen, O.		f8.50
11 f13	94.7	Mercers Bottom		f8.48
11 f17	96.2	Ashton		f8.44
11 f23	98.9	Glenwood		f8.38
11 f31	102.3	Homestead		f8.30
11 f36	104.2	Crown City...Crown City, O.		f8.25
11.40	106.0	Green Bottom		f8.21
11 f46	108.8	Lesage		f8.15
11 f52	111.6	Cox Landing		f8.09
12 f04	117.5	Guyandotte...Proctorsville, O.		f7.57
12.25	120.9	Ar Huntington...Chesapeake, O. Lv		7.35
PM				AM

Ravenswood and Spencer
Daily except Sunday

457 Mixed	Miles	Westward (Read Down)	Eastward (Read Up)	458 Mixed
AM				PM
8.30	0.0	Lv Ravenswood, W. Va. Ar		1.45
f8.38	3.2	Silverton		f1.35
f8.42	4.4	Nuzums		f1.31
f8.45	4.9	Varner		f1.29
f8.52	6.3	Crow Summit		f1.24
f8.55	7.8	New Era		f1.20
f8.58	8.3	Sandyville		f1.17
f9.02	10.0	Murray		f1.09
f9.06	11.0	Jones Crossing		f1.05
f9.13	12.7	Meadowdale		f1.00
f9.17	14.4	Duncan		12 f52
f9.22	15.8	Leroy		12 f47
f9.26	17.1	Liverpool		12 f43
f9.31	18.8	Sandy Summit		12 f37
f9.35	20.0	Sun Flower		12 f27
f9.39	21.0	Seaman		12 f22
f9.41	21.7	Duke		12 f19
f9.46	23.2	Reedy		12 f15
f9.51	24.9	Moore		12 f04
10 f01	27.1	Billings		11 f58
10 f06	28.5	Depue		11 f46
10 f20	30.1	Barr		11 f43
10 f24	31.8	Nancy Run		11 f33
10.30	33.2	Ar Spencer, W. Va. Lv		11.30
AM				AM

Light-face figures A. M. time. **Dark-face figures P. M. time.**
f Stops on signal to receive or discharge passengers.
(EASTERN STANDARD TIME) Form W. 2m. (4-24-60.)

B&O LOCAL TRAIN SERVICE
Parkersburg and Huntington
Train 92—Tuesday, Thursday and Saturday only.
Train 93—Monday, Wednesday and Friday only.

93 Mixed	Miles	Westward (Read Down)	Eastward (Read Up) (Opposite Ohio Towns)	92 Mixed
PM				PM
9.01	0.0	Lv Parkersburg (Fifth St. Sta.)...Belpre, O. Ar		10.22
f9.24	6.1	Washington		f9.58
f9.41	13.6	Harris Ferry...Hockingport, O.		f9.41
f9.50	17.8	Belleville...Reedsville, O.		f9.32
10 f12	27.4	Polk		f9.12
10 f34	34.6	Ravenswood		8.53
10 f59	41.7	Ravenswood Works		8.35
11 f08	45.6	Millwood...Apple Grove, O.		8.22
11 f23	50.6	Letart...Letart Falls, O.		8.11
11 f35	56.1	Graham...Racine, O.		7.47
12 f03	59.4	New Haven...Syracuse, O.		7.40
12 f08	61.1	Hartford...Minersville, O.		7.36
12 f14	63.9	Mason City...Pomeroy, O.		7.30
12 f37	74.3	York		7.05
f1.01	78.9	Point Pleasant...Kanauga, O.		f6.28
f1.25	84.5	Gallipolis...Gallipolis, O.		f6.15
f1.40	90.4	Ben Lomond		f5.54
f1.49	93.9	Apple Grove...Bladen, O.		f5.45
f2.01	98.9	Glenwood		f5.33
f2.14	104.2	Crown City...Crown City, O.		f5.20
f2.33	111.6	Cox Landing		f5.01
f2.46	117.5	Guyandotte...Proctorsville, O.		f4.43
3.06	120.9	Ar Huntington...Chesapeake, O. Lv		4.35
AM				PM

Ravenswood and Spencer
Daily except Sunday

457 Mixed	Miles	Westward (Read Down)	Eastward (Read Up)	458 Mixed
AM				PM
------	7.40	0.0 Lv Ravenswood, W. Va. Ar	12.15	------
------	f8.02	6.3 Crow Summit	11 f53	------
------	f8.08	8.3 Sandyville	11 f47	------
------	f8.23	12.7 Meadowdale	11 f32	------
------	f8.36	17.1 Liverpool	11 f19	------
------	f8.41	18.8 Sandy Summit	11 f14	------
------	f8.56	23.2 Reedy	10 f59	------
------	f9.11	27.1 Billings	10 f44	------
------	9.40	33.2 Ar Spencer, W. Va. Lv	10.15	------
	AM		AM	

Light-face figures A. M. time. **Dark-face figures P. M. time.**
f Stops on signal to receive or discharge passengers.
(EASTERN STANDARD TIME) Form W. 2m. (10-30-60.)

These Form W schedules, issued after the mixed train service along the Ohio River disappeared from the system timetables, illustrate the history of the service in its last years. Local freight Trains 81 and 82 became a mixed train operation in 1932, offered as a concession to the West Virginia Public Service Commission to entice it to approve dropping a pair of passenger trains. Daily-except-Sunday service degenerated to an every-other-day schedule in 1954 and was picked up by overnight freights 92 and 93 (later 103 and 104) in 1960 when 81 and 82 were cut off. The combine didn't last two months on the night trains before being replaced by a caboose. The PSC forced the caboose service to remain – with B&O's grudging compliance – until the advent of Amtrak on May 1, 1971. (Bob Withers Collection)

Posing in front of a festively decorated excursion at the Huntington station in the fall of 1921 are, from left, engineer John Matheny, fireman Roscoe Roush, and conductor Charlie Riggs. The train has just brought hundreds of Parkersburg High School students and chaperones to Huntington for a football game against Huntington High School (Note the football on the front of the engine). This was the first such special sponsored by the Parkersburg Lions Club, and the tradition would continue another 40 years. (Charles S. Ruddell, Bob Withers Collection)

With a member of Train 78's crew looking a bit impatient, Huntington Mayor Walter Payne bids goodbye to the U.S. Army Reserve's 914th Postal Unit on Labor Day, Sept. 4, 1950, before the men leave for Fort Meade, Md., to replace a unit that has been ordered to Korea. The 17 troops will squeeze into sections 6 through 11 of the regular 12-section/drawing room sleeper military style – two men in a lower (except the commander, of course) and one in an upper – for the overnight journey to Pittsburgh. The next morning, the men will race across the Steel City's Monongahela River bridge to catch a connecting train to Washington, D.C. The active-duty call-up will nearly paralyze the Huntington post office and delay deliveries until replacements can be trained. (Lawrence V. Cartmill, Bob Withers Collection)

It's about 7 a.m. on Monday, Feb. 26, 1951, as members of two yard crews and the just-arrived freight Train 93 pose with the Huntington yard engine – Class D-30 0-6-0 1161. On the ground are, from left, day foreman Jess Bagby, night helper Tom Bradbury, night foreman Chester "Shorty" Duvall, 93's flagman Ernie Griffith, and car inspectors George "Tater" Wallace and "Tud" Lykins. Yard engineer Harry Burford is in the cab. (Charles Lemley photo, Bob Withers Collection)

A crowd watches as a Ringling Brothers and Barnum and Bailey circus train arrives in Huntington in 1951. The Baldwin Sharknose is the very first B&O diesel locomotive to enter the city. (Charles Lemley photo, Bob Withers Collection)

A couple of people can be seen milling around inside the Huntington passenger station in this 1953 photograph, even though it is just after 6 a.m. and barely daylight. Train 77 has arrived from Pittsburgh and departed for Kenova – note the sacks of mail on the baggage truck – and mixed Train 82 has picked up its cars and departed for Parkersburg. (Charles Lemley photo, Bob Withers Collection)

A lucky group of Boy Scouts – who, no doubt are working on their railroad merit badges – are about to enjoy a trip to Kenova aboard caboose C1567 on Saturday, April 23, 1955. The man in the dark suit is Chief Clerk Ralph W. Brafford, who will act as trip escort and is instructing the boys on the finer points of special instructions as found in Wheeling Division timetable No. 64. Scoutmaster George "Buzz" Knox listens attentively at right. (Charles Lemley photo, Bob Withers Collection)

Class P-5a Pacific 5220 has brought Train 73 into Huntington on a sunny evening in May 1956. A Railway Express Agency driver prepares to unload packages from the express car as a single passenger – a grandfather, perhaps – walks with his family to their automobile to begin a delightful visit. We don't know about the old gentleman, but the train has less than a year to live. (Herbert H. Harwood Jr. photo, TLC Collection)

The final run of Train 72 stands in Huntington on Jan. 31, 1957. Engineer M.J. "Daddy" Reed, left, and conductor Herbert W. Sammons pose on the ground while freight office clerk Bea Lawwill visits the cab of Class P-6a Pacific 5244. More than 20 retired railroaders and their wives are making the sentimental last journey, many more than No. 72 has carried in several years. The next day, B&O will brag that its passenger service is 100 percent dieselized, ignoring steam-powered mixed Trains 81 and 82 that still operate between Parkersburg and Kenova. (Charles Lemley photo, Bob Withers Collection)

More than 350 business leaders, shippers, and other promi-
nent citizens prepare for an unusual ride on Tuesday, May
12, 1959, sponsored by Huntington's Railroad Community
Committee and the Huntington and Ceredo-Kenova chambers
of commerce to show off business opportunities along local
rights of way. The train, headed by GP9 6551 and including
B&O and C&O coaches and N&W gondolas, will tour the facilities of all three carriers in the Tri-State Area. (Charles Lemley
photo, Bob Withers Collection)

Fireman Harry Nixon poses in the engineer's
seat aboard Class P-6a Pacific 5237 at Ceredo
on Feb. 23, 1954, after the locomotive derailed
at a slow speed on a sharp curve. His colleague
is unidentified. Train 92's engine came up from
Kenova and pulled the coaches away so crews
could rerail the stricken engine, and the train
departed for Wheeling several hours late. The
train was due in Parkersburg at 5:05 p.m., but
Nixon wasn't relieved until 10:05 p.m. (Bob Withers Collection)

This photo of 4-4-0 No. 864 is one of the few we've found of American-type B&O locomotives in West Virginia. The photograph was made at the tiny engine servicing facility in Kenova on Feb. 5, 1932. (TLC Collection)

Train 78 is lined up at Kenova on Tuesday, Nov. 6, 1951, with Class P-5 Pacific 5209, express car 660, baggage-mail RPO 227, coach 5205, and 12-section/drawing room sleeper McElrath. The photograph was taken to present as evidence for the company's first application to the West Virginia Public Service Commission to have Trains 77 and 78 discontinued. The sleeper, ordinarily dropped at Huntington, evidently was taken to Kenova to be included in the picture. (Charles Lemley photo, Bob Withers Collection)

During most of its sunset years, mixed Train 82 consisted only of a steam locomotive and combine for its first eight miles from Kenova to Huntington. It's Tuesday, Aug. 28, 1956, and Class Q-3 MacArthur 4565 will be pulling – with ease – only combine 1397. (TLC Collection)

Even stations that are no longer needed can serve useful purposes, as seen here in May 1959. Clyde Farmer Jr., B&O's smiling district freight agent, hands the Kenova depot's keys to John Kemple, president of the Ceredo-Kenova Chamber of Commerce, for use as a new headquarters. Jimmy Cook, left, of Boy Scout Troop 84, and Larry Hatten, a Civil Defense auxiliary policeman, look on. The small building served as a gathering point for B&O passengers boarding at Kenova during the entire existence of the railroad there, except for a short while in the 1920s when B&O trains called at the Norfolk & Western/ Chesapeake & Ohio Union Depot. The B&O building eventually fell into disrepair in Chamber of Commerce hands and was torn down. [The Huntington Advertiser, Bob Withers Collection)

5: The Pittsburgh Division

B&O's Pittsburgh Division was a major contributor to the company's bottom line. The railroad derived 45 percent of its freight tonnage from bituminous coal and coke, and much of it originated on the Pittsburgh Division. Steel accounted for 10 percent of company revenues, and about 23 percent of that total came from the division as well.

But only two short stretches of Pittsburgh Division track existed on West Virginia soil — the westernmost 12.9 miles of the Wheeling-Pittsburgh line in the Northern Panhandle's Ohio County and the southernmost 32.7 miles of the Fairmont-Connellsville, Pa., line in Monongalia and Marion counties.

B&O launched its first approach to Pittsburgh during the administration of President John W. Garrett with the acquisition of the 32-mile Hempfield Railroad. The line was chartered in 1850 and by the beginning of the Civil War in 1861, it had constructed 32 miles of track between Wheeling and Washington, Pa. After foreclosure, the company was reorganized as the Wheeling, Pittsburgh & Baltimore Railroad and was sold to B&O on May 1, 1871. Garrett, of course, had his eye on the lucrative inbound ore and grain business and outbound coke and steel traffic potentials of Pittsburgh despite having been denied direct access to the city from the east by the political power of the Pennsylvania Railroad and Keystone State politicians. He wanted to extend his new acquisition to a connection with the Pittsburgh & Connellsville Railroad a few miles north of Connellsville. That didn't work out, so B&O eventually reached Pittsburgh from the west in 1883 after Garrett bought the narrow-gauge 37-mile Pittsburgh Southern Railroad. He widened its track in some places, rebuilt it on new alignments in others, and connected it with the B&O-controlled P&C at Glenwood, Pa.

In the 1890s during the administration of President Charles F. Mayer, B&O bought the 63-mile FM&P line — which offered plenty of revenue from coal mining. Morgantown and Star City, W.Va., provided additional traffic in chemicals and glassware. Later, this route would serve as a viable detour whenever a derailment blocked the Cumberland Division's mountainous west end.

The fireman aboard Extra 3500 East stands on the front end of his GP35 to receive orders from the operator at the Morgantown station on the Fairmont-Connellsville, Pa., line on Sept. 27, 1969. (Thomas W. Dixon Jr. photo)

F7 No. 4539 leads an A-B-A diesel trio through Tridelphia, a small town 7.6 miles from the Pennsylvania border on the Wheeling-Pittsburgh line. It's 1972, and the lead unit's paint job is showing its age. (TLC Collection)

The Baltimore & Ohio Railroad provided West Virginia with quality passenger service for decades. The best-known runs through the Mountain State, of course, were the flagship *National Limited* and its lesser running mates, the *Diplomat* and *Metropolitan Special*, on their daily trips between Jersey City, N.J., and St. Louis. Also deserving honorable mention is the Baltimore-Cincinnati *Cincinnatian*, which crisscrossed northern West Virginia between January 1947 and June 1950 before being shifted to a Cincinnati-Detroit run. The Jersey City-Chicago flagship *Capitol Limited* and its running mates, the *Columbian*, *Ambassador*, *Shenandoah* and the *Washington* and *Chicago Expresses*, served the state's Eastern Panhandle as well — as did the *Cleveland Night Express* and the Rail Diesel Car-equipped *Daylight Speedliner* to Pittsburgh.

But, at one time or another, B&O also fielded passenger runs on nearly every branch line in West Virginia as well — included some of the shortest ones (the 6.1-mile Berkeley Springs line and the 12.3-mile Ripley & Mill Creek Valley branch come to mind). Many of those trains fell victim to the Great Depression, and many more disappeared after World War II as riders deserted them for the private automobile and air travel.

For a while, though, some of those branch-line trains offered amenities such as sleepers, diners, parlor cars and lounges. A passenger train consist book from 1917 lists among the company's dozens of Pullman car lines several of special interest to West Virginians — such as Jersey City-Parkersburg, Huntington-Parkersburg (eastbound only), Parkersburg-Washington (eastbound only), Parkersburg to Pittsburgh (eastbound only), Pittsburgh-Clarksburg and Pittsburgh-Huntington. Passengers boarding in Wheeling also could go Pullman to Cincinnati, Chicago, Washington and Huntington. One westbound-only Pullman line went from Baltimore to Pittsburgh via Grafton, Fairmont, Morgantown and Connellsville, Pa.

A public timetable issued on Sept. 30, 1923, after B&O had acquired a few more Mountain State holdings, listed a Pittsburgh-Charleston line that twisted eastward to Connellsville, Pa.; southward to Morgan-

The eastbound National Limited *is crossing from Harpers Ferry into Maryland in the late 1920s. The train was all-Pullman west of Washington, D.C., and featured a Pullman-operated baggage/club car staffed with a barber/valet, maid/manicurist and train secretary. Parlor cars ran during daylight hours between Jersey City and Washington and between Cincinnati and St. Louis. Colonial diners offered Georgian leaded windows, Sheraton sideboards and high-back Hepplewhite chairs. (TLC Collection)*

town and Fairmont; southwesternly over to Clarksburg; eastward to Grafton; and southward again through Buckhannon, Burnsville and Gassaway!

Also, by 1923, Trains 77-78 on the Pittsburgh-to-Kenova route carried Pittsburgh-Huntington, Parkersburg-Huntington and Parkersburg-Charleston sleepers — the latter traveling on the Chesapeake & Ohio Railway between Huntington and Charleston. That line eventually was extended on the C&O to Hinton, W.Va. The Parkersburg-Huntington sleeper was gone by 1932; the Pittsburgh-Huntington sleeper was dropped in 1942. The Pittsburgh-Hinton sleeper was cut back to Huntington in 1949 and disappeared with its trains in 1953.

Alas, that was the wave of the future. Sleeping car service lasted on the *National Limited* east of Parkersburg until the spring of 1968, and the *Capitol Limited* kept its sleepers until the final eastbound Train No. 6 arrived in Washington, D.C., on May 1, 1971 — Amtrak Day.

Another West Virginia "passenger service" lasted until Amtrak Day — caboose mixed trains 103 and 104 between Parkersburg and Huntington, the last remnant of "service" on the Wheeling Division's Ohio River Line.

Amtrak tried, ultimately in vain, to operate passenger service through northern West Virginia on three or four separate occasions — including a short-lived and little known experiment with coaches equipped with "sleeper sections" that looked like curtained, double-stack glass coffins. The last passenger service on B&O lines in West Virginia – except in the eastern panhandle – succumbed for good in 1981.

This page in The Official Guide, thought to be from the mid-1930s, shows that, of all the trains B&O could choose to advertise, it selected the National Limited. *The train was a big hit with the traveling public and government officials before jet air travel, the private automobile and interstate highways came along. (TLC Collection)*

B&O's 52-page timetable issued on Sept. 25, 1949, with its simple and familiar royal blue and white cover, published passenger schedules covering virtually every point in West Virginia served by the company.

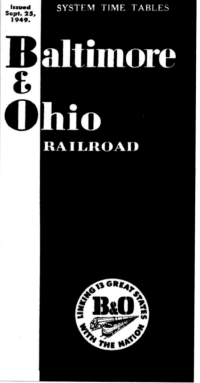

Issued Sept. 25, 1949.

SYSTEM TIME TABLES

Baltimore & Ohio

RAILROAD

LINKING 13 GREAT STATES WITH THE NATION — B&O

371

BALTIMORE & OHIO RAILROAD
The National Limited
COMPLETELY AIR-CONDITIONED
NEW YORK-PHILADELPHIA-BALTIMORE-WASHINGTON-CINCINNATI-LOUISVILLE-ST. LOUIS
No Extra Fare

Club Car and through Sleepers between New York and St. Louis. Sun-room Observation-Lounge Car; Sleepers (Compartments, Drawing-rooms); Dining Cars, Reclining Seat Coaches, Train Secretary, Barber--Valet, Maid--Manicure and Shower Baths, between Washington and St. Louis.

including New York, N.Y.; Jersey City, N.J.; Newark, N.J.; Elizabeth, N.J., and & Pittsburgh Railway and the Buffalo and Susquehanna Corporation.

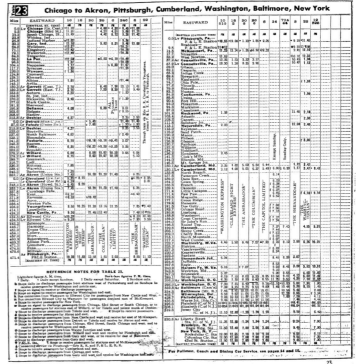

Table 22 — New York, Baltimore, Washington to Cumberland, Pittsburgh, Akron, Chicago

Table 23 — Chicago to Akron, Pittsburgh, Cumberland, Washington, Baltimore, New York

As this Sept. 25, 1949, schedule shows, B&O's Jersey City-Chicago trains served West Virginia points between Harpers Ferry and Cumberland, Md. (Bob Withers Collection)

Class P-7e Pacific 5315 charges out of the Mountain State at Harpers Ferry with Train 34, the Cumberland-Washington local, in the early 1950s. If the long train is on time, it's 9:19 a.m. The engineer offers the photographer a big wave; maybe he's proud that his train is one of the last powered by steam east of Cumberland. (James P. Gallagher photo, TLC Collection)

Opposite This retouched company photo shows the westbound Daylight Speedliner crossing into Harpers Ferry. The train, using three self-propelled Rail Diesel Cars, ran between Philadelphia and Pittsburgh from Oct. 28, 1956, to April 26, 1958, and between Baltimore and Pittsburgh from April 27, 1958, to Jan. 21, 1963. The Budd cars featured reclining seats instead of straight-back commuter seats and baggage compartments remodeled into kitchen and dining areas. (Lawrence S. Williams photo, TLC Collection)

Westbound Train 5, the Chicago section of the Capitol Limited, *rumbles across the Potomac River bridge at Harpers Ferry on Aug. 13, 1966. A 43-day airline strike has swelled its consist to 21 cars. The Chicago and Detroit sections of the streamliner, normally combined east of Willard, Ohio, are running separately for the duration. (Railroad Avenue Enterprises)*

Pullman-built dome/coach lounge 5550, originally named High Dome *and assigned to the restyled* Columbian *in 1949, is a part of the long* Capitol Limited *stopping at Harpers Ferry on Aug. 13, 1966. (Railroad Avenue Enterprises)*

Slumberland (car 7700) is probably full of grounded airline passengers as the westbound Capitol Limited *comes to a stop at Harpers Ferry on Aug. 13, 1966. It and the identical* Dreamland *(car 7701) were B&O's first foray into the Slumbercoach business. The Budd-built cars each featured 24 single rooms and eight double rooms, offering private sleeping spaces for regular coach fares plus a small room charge. The bold move, designed to retain or increase sleeping-car patronage, generally failed. After the airline strike was settled, passenger counts resumed their downward spiral despite the bargain. (Railroad Avenue Enterprises)*

Train 9, the Chicago Express, *pulls into Martinsburg on June 27, 1964, at 3:38 p.m. (if it's on time). The Baltimore-Chicago run still offers an enjoyable experience for travelers boarding here – reclining-seat coaches, a dining/lounge car, and a 16-duplex roomette/4-double bedroom "Bird"-series sleeping car. The train will pick up a 10-roomette/6-double bedroom sleeper at Pittsburgh for the nighttime portion of its trip. (Railroad Avenue Enterprises)*

Westbound Train 11, the Metropolitan Special, *prepares to depart Martinsburg on April 28, 1954. Through passengers from the East are likely finishing their breakfasts before the diner is cut off at Cumberland, and new arrivals heading for St. Louis probably are settling into their unmade berths or maybe even the drawing room. (TLC Collection)*

Class P-7 Pacific 5320 charges out of Hancock with a nine-car Metropolitan Special *in the late morning hours of March 16, 1947. Through passengers will be in St. Louis at about breakfast time tomorrow. (E.L. Thompson photo, B&O RR Historical Society Collection)*

Train 9, known at the time as the Washington-Pittsburgh-Chicago Express *and running on the original main line, passes under the Magnolia Cutoff at Magnolia on May 7, 1952. Passengers in the 8-section/buffet/lounge car are undoubtedly enjoying the view, scarfing down a snack or listening to the radio. (William P. Price photo)*

Here comes Class P-1d Pacific 5066 with eastbound Train 22, the Washingtonian, *also at Magnolia, on Oct. 16, 1952. The* Washingtonians *were daylight trains between Baltimore and Cleveland which used P&LE and Erie tracks west of Pittsburgh. (William P. Price photo)*

E6 diesel 63 and another unit charge through Green Spring with Train 9, the westbound Washington-Pittsburgh-Chicago Express, *on April 6, 1947. (William P. Price photo)*

Class P-1d Pacific 5003 charges through Patterson Creek with a seven-car eastbound passenger train on July 29, 1948. Information on the back of the photo post card says it's No. 2, but we doubt that. The National Limited *was one of the St. Louis line trains that bypassed Cumberland, Md., via the Patterson Creek Cutoff, which is visible in the foreground. (H. Kindig photo)*

E6 diesel 64 leads No. 9, the westbound Washington-Pittsburgh-Chicago Express, *through Patterson Creek on the afternoon of April 26, 1947. (William P. Price photo)*

Streamlined Class P-7d Pacific 5304 approaches Patterson Creek with Train 75, the westbound Cincinnatian, on Oct. 13, 1949. The five-car streamliner, which used rebuilt heavyweight cars, was a noble experiment inaugurated in January 1947 to provide a fast daylight train between Baltimore, Washington and Cincinnati. But after three and a half years of operation, the company decided that the luxury train wouldn't work on that route and shifted it to the flat Cincinnati-Detroit corridor. The problem was that maintaining a 12-hour schedule precluded the use of helpers, extra coaches and revenue-producing mail and express cars. Incidentally, the 5304 received a shroud once before and only briefly – for operation of the Jersey City-Washington Royal Blue, from 1937 to 1940. (William P. Price photo, Bob Withers Collection)

Table 24 — New York, Washington to Parkersburg, Cincinnati, Louisville, St. Louis

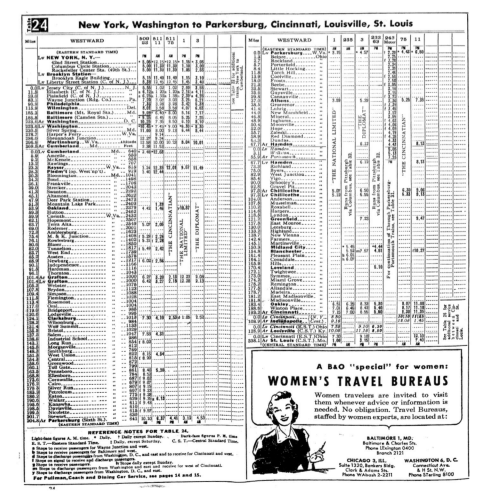

REFERENCE NOTES FOR TABLE 24.

Light-face figures A. M. time. • Daily. ‡ Daily except Sunday. Dark-face figures P. M. time
E. S. T.—Eastern Standard Time. ‡ Daily, except Saturday. C. S. T.—Central Standard Time.
a Stops to receive passengers for Wayne Junction and west.
b Stops to receive passengers for Baltimore and west.
c Stops to discharge passengers from Washington, D. C., and west and to receive for Cincinnati and west.
d Stops on signal to receive and discharge passengers.
g Stops to receive passengers. h Stops daily except Sunday.
m Stops to discharge passengers from Washington and east and to receive for west of Cincinnati.
y Stops to discharge passengers from Washington, D. C., and east.
For Pullman, Coach and Dining Car Service, see pages 14 and 15.

A B&O "special" for women:
WOMEN'S TRAVEL BUREAUS

Women travelers are invited to visit them whenever advice or information is needed. No obligation. Travel Bureaus, staffed by women experts, are located at:

BALTIMORE 1, MD.
Baltimore & Charles Bldg.
Phone LExington 0400
Branch 2121

CHICAGO 3, ILL.
Suite 1320, Bankers Bldg.
Clark & Adams Sts.
Phone WAbash 2-2211

WASHINGTON 6, D. C.
Connecticut Ave.
& H St. N.W.
Phone STerling 8100

E7 diesel 74 and a B-unit hustle Train 8, the eastbound Shenandoah, *through Patterson Creek on Oct. 13, 1949. The train suffered from a bit of an identity crisis through the years, being known sometimes as the* Shenandoah *and at other times the Diplomat. (William P. Price photo)*

Right and Opposite: These pages from the Sept. 25, 1949, timetable give an idea of the company's passenger service offered at the time between Harpers Ferry and Parkersburg on the St. Louis line. (Bob Withers Collection)

Table 25 — St. Louis, Louisville, Cincinnati to Parkersburg, Washington, New York

(Left table — EASTWARD; trains 944 Motor, 76, 12, 938, 2, 4, 236)

Miles	EASTWARD		
	(CENTRAL STANDARD TIME)		
0.0	Lv St. LOUIS (C.S.T.) Mo.		
338.1	Ar Cincinnati (E.S.T.) Ohio		
0.0	Lv Louisville (C.S.T.) Ky.		
128.0	Ar Cincinnati (E.S.T.) Ohio		
0.0	Lv Indianapolis (N.Y. Cent.)		
108.0	Ar Cincinnati, O. (N.Y. Cent.)		
0.0	Lv Cincinnati (E.S.T.) Ohio		
4.6	Winton Place		
9.6	Oakley		
11.4	Madisonville		
14.0	East Madisonville		
15.9	Madeira		
15.7	Ailandale		
18.0	Remington		
19.0	Miami Grove		
20.2	Symmes		
21.1	Twightwee		
22.8	Loveland		
27.3	Hille		
29.1	Cozaddale		
31.8	Pleasant Plain		
35.7	Blanchester		
42.9	Midland City		
48.1	Martinsville		
50.8	Farmers		
64.8	New Vienna		
68.2	Leesburg		
80.4	East Monroe		
72.0	Greenfield		
74.7	Lyndon		
78.0	Harpers		
83.0	Roxabell		
88.7	Musselman		
89.2	Anderson		
95.9	Ar Chillicothe		
95.9	Lv Chillicothe		
100.4	Gravel Pit		
103.2	Schooley's		
107.8	Vigo		
110.3	West Junction		
118.2	Byers		
119.0	Richland		
123.5	Ar Hamden		
42.8	Lv Portsmouth		
52.8	Ar Wellston		
65.9	Ar Hamden		
125.5	Lv Hamden		
129.0	Dundas		
134.5	Red Diamond		
137.6	Zaleski		
141.2	Hope		
142.3	Moonville		
144.3	Ingham		
148.2	Mineral		
149.3	New Marshfield		
151.8	Luhrig		
154.7	Grosvenor		
156.2	Athens		
163.4	Canaanville		
167.0	Guysville		
169.7	Stewart		
171.9	Beebe		
175.1	Frost		
179.3	Coolville		
181.4	Torch Hill		
184.8	Little Hocking		
187.5	Porterfield		
190.5	Rockland		
191.9	Belpre		
193.2	Ar PARKERSBURG W.Va.		
	(EASTERN STANDARD TIME)		

(Right table — EASTWARD; trains 4, 30/8, 76, 12/528, 24/10/510, 2)

Miles	EASTWARD		
0.0	(Sixth St. Station) Lv Parkersburg W.Va.	Altitude Feet 641	
3.1	Stewart	630	
5.3	Nicolette	615	
6.3	Davisville	610	
14.2	Kanawha	611	
14.8	Walker	629	
18.6	Eaton	775	
21.6	Petroleum	697	
26.5	Silver Run	807	
28.5	Cairo	679	
31.2	Cornwallis	687	
36.0	Ellenboro	784	
41.3	Pennsboro	861	
44.7	Toll Gate	799	
46.2	Greenwood	872	
50.5	Central	815	
53.5	West Union	824	
56.5	Smithburg	769	
59.3	Morganville	812	
61.7	Long Run	854	
66.5	Industrial School	986	
67.3	Salem	1017	
69.3	Bristol	1029	
73.4	Wolf Summit	1133	
77.6	Wilsonburg	984	
80.7	Clarksburg	1013	
84.2	Lodgeville	995	
86.8	Bridgeport	985	
91.4	Rosemont	1004	
93.3	Flemington	1028	
95.4	Simpson	1088	
101.9	Ar Grafton	1000	
103.4	Lv Grafton	1000	
108.7	Thornton	1043	
113.3	Hardman	1116	
114.7	Independence	1166	
116.9	Newburg	1317	
119.6	Austen	1575	
121.1	West End	1729	
122.8	Tunnelton	1817	
124.2	Blaser	1850	
126.7	Rowlesburg	1402	
129.4	M. & K. Junction	1408	
132.5	Ambersburg	1623	
136.8	Rodemer	2001	
141.1	Terra Alta	2548	
142.7	Hopemont	2432	
144.9	Corinth	2432	
145.5	Hutton	2462	
150.0	Oakland Md.	2379	
153.5	Mountain Lake Park	2433	
154.5	Deer Park Station	2473	
159.7	Altamont	2628	
163.5	Swanton	2292	
165.4	Strecker	2043	
167.7	Frankville	1706	
170.5	Bond	1498	
173.0	Bloomington	1041	
176.5	Piedm't (op. West p'O) W.Va.	919	
180.0	Keyser	815	
186.0	Dawson Md.	758	
191.6	Rawlings	707	
195.6	McKenzie	650	
198.9	Amcelle	640	
204.8	Ar Cumberland Md.		
277.4	Lv Cumberland		
289.3	Martinsburg W.Va.		
293.6	Shenandoah Junction		
295.6	Harper's Ferry		
343.8	Silver Spring Md.		
350.7	Ar Washington D.C.		
350.7	Lv Washington		
387.5	Ar Baltimore (Camden Sta.) Md.		
389.0	Baltimore (Mt. Royal Sta.)		
458.4	Wilmington Del.		
465.4	Philadelphia Pa.		
491.2	Wayne Junction (Rdg. Co.)		
551.3	Plainfield (C. of N. J.) N.J.		
562.8	Elizabeth (C. of N. J.)		
574.3	Ar Jersey City (C. of N. J.)		
575.3	Ar Liberty Street Station (C. of N.J.)		
	Brooklyn Station		
	Brooklyn Eagle Building		
	Ar NEW YORK, N.Y. —		
	Rockefeller Center Sta. (49th St.)		
	Columbus Circle Station		
	42d Street Station		
	(EASTERN STANDARD TIME)		

REFERENCE NOTES FOR TABLE 25.

Light-face figures A. M. time. • Daily. † Daily except Sunday. Dark-face figures P. M. time.
C. T.—Central Standard Time. E. T.—Eastern Standard Time.
e Stops to receive passengers for Martinsburg and east.
f Stops on signal to receive or discharge passengers.
t Stops to receive passengers from west of Parkersburg and receive for Washington and east.
h Stops daily except Sunday.
s Stops to discharge passengers from Wayne Junction and west.
t Stops to discharge passengers from Baltimore and west.
w Stops daily from west of Parkersburg, and on Sundays to receive passengers for Washington and east.
x Stops to receive passengers from west of Cincinnati, and receive for Washington and east.
z Stops to discharge passengers from Clarksburg and west
Note 6—Train 30 will stop on signal at Leamlatoint, Irontown, Hiorrs, Wilson and Potomac.
For Pullman, Coach and Dining Car Service, see pages 14 and 15.

PARMELEE OFFERS YOU THIS SERVICE IN CHICAGO —

...IF YOU HOLD A THROUGH TICKET WITH PARMELEE COUPON

A Parmelee agent will meet your incoming train and arrange for a new, luxurious Limousine to carry you
—to your outgoing railway station
—or to any hotel or other destination in Chicago's downtown District

WITHOUT EXTRA CHARGE

Any Railway Ticket Agent will be glad to tell you about Parmelee service.

25

A three-unit freight diesel led by F7 287 pulls mail-and-express train 29 across the Maryland-West Virginia state line 2.2 miles east of Keyser on July 3, 1952. (William P. Price photo, TLC Collection)

Class P-7d Pacific 5301 departs Keyser with Train 75, the westbound Cincinnatian, on July 27, 1947. The train used the Patterson Creek Cutoff around Cumberland, Md., generating a good bit of grumbling from Cumberland folks who had to drive to Keyser to catch the spiffy little streamliner. (Bob's Photo, B&O RR Historical Society Collection)

We're in the mountains now. Two F units and two E units forward Train 11, the westbound Metropolitan Special, through Hopemont on Sept. 14, 1964. (Martin S. Zak photo, TLC Collection)

Class P-1d Pacific 5036 takes Train 11, the westbound Metropolitan Special, down Cranberry Grade at Amblersburg on April 2, 1950. Baldwin built the locomotive as Class Q-1 Mikado 4138 in 1911. It was reclassified as a Q-1a when it received a superheater in 1916 and as a Q-1aa in 1923 when it received outside steam pipes and a new firebox with an increased heating surface. Mount Clare shops in Baltimore rebuilt the engine as Class P-1c Pacific 5036 in 1924 and it was reclassified as a P-1d six years later. It was taken out of service on Dec. 29, 1953. (B&O RR Historical Society Collection)

Class Q-4b MacArthur 4476 and Class P-1aa Pacific 5076 take westbound Train 30 out of Amblersburg in 1945. (H.W. Pontin photo, Herbert H. Harwood Jr. Collection)

Class Q-4b MacArthur 4476 and Class P-1d Pacific 5056 make a run for Cranberry Grade on Train 30 with seven cars east of M&K Junction on July 26, 1949. (B&O RR Historical Society Collection)

Train 12, the eastbound Metropolitan Special, with Class Q-4b MacArthur 4476 and Class P-1d Pacific 5085 for power, passes R Tower at the west end of M&K Junction on June 12, 1949. The tower, built in 1913 as maybe the widest such structure on the B&O, housed 68 armstrong levers and required three men on each shift to function – operator, lever man and hill supervisor. That hill supervisor – possibly a unique position on the railroad – scheduled returning helper movements on the Cranberry, Cheat and Newburg Grades; there were so many such movements that the Cumberland Division dispatcher couldn't handle them all. The old building and its plant were replaced in 1954 by a brick tower and a modernized interlocking plant, which was designated MK Tower. (W.H. Thrall photo, TLC Collection)

E8 diesel 1439 and E7 mate 1424 take Train 12, the eastbound Metropolitan, through M&K Junction on No. 1 track on May 5, 1966. Note there are six mail and express cars and a single coach. (F.R. Kern photo, Jay Potter Collection)

Class Q-4b MacArthur 4463 and Class P-1d Pacific 5043 take No. 11, the westbound Metropolitan Special, across the Cheat River bridge between M&K Junction and Rowlesburg on April 13, 1947. It should be obvious by now that since Trains 11 and 12 operated through the West Virginian mountains in daylight hours, many more photos were taken of them than of other top-grade runs on the St. Louis line like the National Limited and Diplomat. (E.L. Thompson photo, B&O RR Historical Society Collection)

E6 diesel 57 brings a seven-car No. 11, the westbound Metropolitan Special, into Rowlesburg on July 21, 1951, where several passengers are waiting. Behind the locomotive and several trees stands Mrs. Annette Howard's 13-room New Howard Hotel, where many a fan, B&O officer, historian, and foreign visitor was nourished by her succulent stewed tomatoes and rocked to sleep by the sounds and smells of railroading. (TLC Collection)

Train 75, the westbound Cincinnatian, crosses Tray Run Viaduct on Cheat River Grade west of Rowlesburg sometime between Jan. 19, 1947, its first run, and June 24, 1950, after which it was transferred to the Cincinnati-Detroit route. The graceful 443-foot-long stone structure, which replaced a spindly but elegant earlier span in 1888, consisted of four 90-foot arches. (B&O RR Historical Society Collection)

Class P-1d Pacific 5085 advances No. 11, the westbound Metropolitan Special, past K Tower at Blaser, near the top of Cheat River Grade, on June 11, 1949. The tower was built in about 1912 and was active until late 1956, after which its functions were handled from West End Tower, on the west side of the Kingwood Tunnel bores, and later, from MK Tower east of Rowlesburg. (W.H. Thrall photo, TLC Collection)

Streamlined Class P-7d Pacific 5301 is about the take Train 75, the westbound Cincinnatian, into the original bore of Kingwood Tunnel on the "high line" just west of Tunnelton at 1:44 p.m. May 11, 1949. Getting trains over the summit of Laurel Mountain proved to be an exercise in patience for the company. Beginning when the line opened in 1853, extremely short trains – like one car each – were operated over the top on a grade that reached 10 percent. The original 4,254-foot-long tunnel finally opened in 1857, after considerable construction problems. The newer double-tracked 4,201-foot-long bore, the eastern approach to which is seen in this photo, was completed in 1912 and exited on the eastern side about 24 feet below the old tunnel. That enabled helpers to cut off before entering the choking darkness. The old single-track tunnel was taken out of service in 1956 and plugged at both ends in 1962. (Bruce D. Fales photo, Jay Williams Collection)

Class Q-4b MacArthur 4464 and Class P-1d Pacific 5043 haul the seven cars of No. 11, the westbound Metropolitan Special, through Newburg on June 29, 1947. From here to Hardman, the downhill grade won't be as steep. (E.L. Thompson photo, B&O RR Historical Society Collection)

The Cincinnatian rolls easily through Thornton, 5.3 miles east of Grafton near the foot of Newburg Grade. The stack is clear; the fireman knows his stuff. (B&O RR Historical Society Collection)

Class T3t Mountain 5579, pulling seven mail and express cars and a single coach on Train 30, departs Grafton on June 9, 1955. Baltimore's Mount Clare Shops built the 4-8-2 in 1945, adding it to several already cobbled together from old Pacifics and MacArthurs in 1943 and '44, to forward wartime freight and passengers more efficiently. By 1948, the company had produced 40 of these powerful locomotives, the last batch of engines ever built at Mount Clare. The "t" in the classification refers to the long tender recovered from an out-of-service 2-8-8-0. (William P. Price photo, TLC Collection)

A C&O E8 brings a five-car Train 12, the eastbound Metropolitan, into Grafton in November 1969. This picture offers a good look at the station and former Willard Hotel, then in use as a rest house for crews. The three-story, 16,000-square foot Beaux Art station, Grafton's third passenger depot, cost the company $125,000 when it was built in 1911. The matching seven-story hotel – complete with its impressive restaurant, dining halls, ballroom and barber shop – opened a year later. (TLC Collection)

The last run of Train 32, the eastbound West Virginian, calls at Grafton for the final time on Aug. 23, 1969, with E8 1452 and a single coach. The last remnant of the National Limited is dying an agonizing death. Notice that the umbrella sheds are gone. Passenger service under Amtrak would resume in fits and starts for a while, before ending permanently in 1981. (Lloyd D. Lewis photo, Bob Withers Collection)

Moving slightly west of the Grafton station, we see E8 1444 bringing a three-car Train 12, the eastbound Metropolitan, past D Tower on June 9, 1968. (F.R. Kern photo, Jay Potter Collection)

Class P-1c 5039 and Class P-1ba 5080 takes Train 11, the westbound Metropolitan Special, out of Grafton on Aug. 15, 1947. The Pacifics are passing the old Grafton passenger station that was located between the old main line to Fairmont and the Parkersburg Branch that became the "new main line" when it opened in 1857. The building served other purposes until it was torn down a few years later. (Howard N. Barr Sr. photo, TLC Collection)

E7a 65 and a B unit are taking No. 11 out of Grafton on Aug. 8, 1951. The old station building appears to be gone. (E.L. Thompson photo, B&O RR Historical Society Collection)

Train 75, the westbound Cincinnatian, crosses the Tygart Valley River bridge in Grafton on Oct. 18, 1947. One of the four Pacifics streamlined for this train is doing the work. (B&O RR Historical Society Collection)

Class P-7c Pacific 5317 brings Train 76, the eastbound Cincinnatian, across the Tygart Valley River bridge in Grafton on July 27, 1947. Non-streamlined engines sometimes substituted for the more glamorous members of their class for one reason or another. (R.H. Kindig photo, B&O RR Historical Society Collection)

This picture shows the Tygart Valley River bridge in more detail. Class P-1d Pacific 5049 is on the point of No. 11 at 2:29 p.m. July 27, 1949. (Bruce D. Fales, Jay Williams Collection)

Mail-and-express Train 29 calls at Clarksburg on Aug. 8, 1951. It looks like the station work is done and the train is ready to leave for Parkersburg on the westbound main. (E.L. Thompson photo, B&O RR Historical Society Collection)

E7 diesel 1416 is leading train 11, the westbound Metropolitan Special, through the streets of St. Marys on June 21, 1963. The National Limited and the Metropolitan Special are being detoured via New Martinsville on the Short Line and Ohio River subdivisions to bypass a months-long tunnel enlargement/elimination project on the Clarksburg-Parkersburg main line. Eastbound motorists must be extremely vigilant – there isn't enough room between the train and parked cars for vehicles moving on that side of the street. (S. Durward Hoag photo, TLC Collection)

Train 1, the westbound National Limited, stands at Parkersburg on Sept. 1, 1940. There are signs of trouble: The streamliner is running in daylight, several hours late, and it has double-headed steam power on the head end rather than diesels. It's possible the train has been detoured around a derailment somewhere back East. It looks like crews are preparing to detach Class P-5 helper 5220 from the road engine as the tardy train prepares to fly across the relatively flat and straight profile through southern Ohio. (S.P. Davidson photo, Bob Withers Collection)

WESTWARD.

Cowen Sub-Division.
TIME-TABLE No. 65.
April 26, 1953.

Mile Post Location	Train Order Stations	FIRST CLASS		THIRD CLASS				
		135 DAILY Sunday	453 DAILY Sunday	83 DAILY	91 DAILY	95 P.M.	81 P.M.	99 P.M.

(Westward timetable, Cowen Sub-Division, stations from BERKELEY RUN JCT. 0.0 to WN TOWER 116.5, including KNIGHT, PLEASANT CREEK, BERRYBURG JCT., PHILIPPI, TYGART JCT., CENTURY JCT., HALL, TETER, SMITH SUMMIT, POST MILL, BUCKHANNON, UPSHUR, HAMPTON JCT., ADRIAN, ABBOTT, FRENCHTON, CRAWFORD, WALKERSVILLE, CHAPMAN, ORLANDO, BURNSVILLE JCT., BURNSVILLE, COGER, ROLLYSON, HEATERS, FLATWOODS, GILLESPIE, HOLLY, BAKERS RUN, CENTRALIA, PRESTONIA, ERBACON, HARDWOOD, HALO, WN TOWER.)

Passenger trains will not exceed 35 miles per hour, Berkeley Run Jct. and Burnsville Junction; 20 miles per hour, Burnsville Junction and Heaters; 30 miles per hour, Heaters and Centralia; 20 miles per hour, Centralia and Halo; 30 miles per hour, Halo and WN Tower.

Speed as shown in Special Instruction 5, and such other restrictions as may be in effect, will not be exceeded.

16   Monongah Div.

EASTWARD.

Cowen Sub-Division.
TIME-TABLE No. 65.
April 26, 1953.

Mile Post Location	Train Order Stations	FIRST CLASS		THIRD CLASS				
		454 DAILY Sunday	136 DAILY Sunday	98 DAILY	82 DAILY	86 P.M.	80 P.M.	92 P.M.

(Eastward timetable, Cowen Sub-Division, stations from WN TOWER 116.5 to BERKELEY RUN JCT. 0.0.)

Passenger trains will not exceed 30 miles per hour, WN Tower and Halo; 20 miles per hour, Halo and Centralia; 30 miles per hour, Centralia and Heaters; 20 miles per hour, Heaters and Burnsville Junction; 35 miles per hour, Burnsville Jct. and Berkeley Run Jct.

Speed as shown in Special Instruction 5, and such other restrictions as may be in effect, will not be exceeded.

17   Monongah Div.

These pages, taken from the Monongah Division timetable issued in the spring of 1953, offer a good idea of how busy the Grafton-Cowen line was at the time. Except for the passenger trains, the multiple schedules continued well into the 1960s. (Bob Withers Collection)

There were fewer trains on the West End than the East End of the Ohio River Subdivision, so all the schedules in both directions that were placed in effect on Sept. 25, 1949, could be placed on two pages instead of four. (Bob Withers Collection)

WESTWARD.

Ohio River. West End.
TIME-TABLE No. 53.
September 25, 1949.

Distance from Wheeling	Train Order Stations	FIRST CLASS		SECOND CLASS			THIRD CLASS
		77 DAILY	73 DAILY	961 DAILY Sunday	81 Ex. Sunday	457 Ex. Sunday	93 DAILY

(Westward timetable, Ohio River West End, stations from PARKERSBURG 93.8 to KENOVA 222.9, including O. R. JCT., WASHINGTON, HARRIS FERRY, BELLEVILLE, POLK, RAVENSWOOD, R. S. & G. JCT., WILLOW GROVE, MILLWOOD, RIPLEY, LETART, GRAHAM, NEW HAVEN, HARTFORD, MASON CITY, KROY, YORK, BADEN, POINT PLEASANT, GALLIPOLIS, BEN LOMOND, APPLE GROVE, GLENWOOD, CROWN CITY, COX LANDING, GUYANDOTTE, HUNTINGTON, WEST HUNTINGTON, KENOVA.)

R. S. & G. Sub-Division.
TIME-TABLE No. 53.
September 25, 1949.

Distance from R. S. & G. Junction	Train Order Stations	SECOND CLASS —WESTWARD	THIRD CLASS
		457 DAILY Ex. Sunday	

(Stations R. S. & G. JCT. 0.0, CROW SUMMIT, SANDYVILLE, MEADOWDALE, LIVERPOOL, SANDY SUMMIT, REEDY, BILLINGS, SPENCER.)

Passenger trains will not exceed 45 miles per hour between Kenova and Parkersburg, and 20 miles per hour between Ripley and Millwood.
Passenger trains will not exceed 20 miles per hour between R. S. & G. Junction and Spencer.
Speed as shown in Special Instruction 5, and such other restrictions as may be in effect, will not be exceeded.
Trains Nos. 81, 961 and 457 will carry passengers.

14   Wheeling Div.

EASTWARD.

Ohio River. West End.
TIME-TABLE No. 53.
September 25, 1949.

Distance from Kenova	Train Order Stations	FIRST CLASS		SECOND CLASS			THIRD CLASS
		72 DAILY	78 DAILY	962 DAILY Sunday	82 Ex. Sunday	458 Ex. Sunday	92 DAILY

(Eastward timetable, Ohio River West End, stations from KENOVA 0.0 to PARKERSBURG 129.1, including WEST HUNTINGTON, HUNTINGTON, GUYANDOTTE, COX LANDING, CROWN CITY, GLENWOOD, APPLE GROVE, BEN LOMOND, GALLIPOLIS, POINT PLEASANT, BADEN, YORK, KROY, MASON CITY, HARTFORD, NEW HAVEN, GRAHAM, LETART, RIPLEY, MILLWOOD, WILLOW GROVE, R. S. & G. JCT., RAVENSWOOD, POLK, BELLEVILLE, HARRIS FERRY, WASHINGTON, O. R. JCT., PARKERSBURG.)

R. S. & G. Sub-Division.
TIME-TABLE No. 53.
September 25, 1949.

Distance from Spencer	Train Order Stations	SECOND CLASS —EASTWARD	THIRD CLASS
		458 DAILY Ex. Sunday	

(Stations SPENCER 0.0, BILLINGS, REEDY, SANDY SUMMIT, LIVERPOOL, MEADOWDALE, SANDYVILLE, CROW SUMMIT, R. S. & G. JCT.)

Passenger trains will not exceed 45 miles per hour between Kenova and Parkersburg and 20 miles per hour between Ripley and Millwood.
Passenger trains will not exceed 20 miles per hour between R. S. & G. Junction and Spencer.
Speed as shown in Special Instruction 5, and such other restrictions as may be in effect, will not be exceeded.
Train 72 stops on flag at Hartford and Letart to discharge passengers from Point Pleasant and west and pick up passengers for Parkersburg and beyond. Trains Nos. 82-962 and 458 will carry passengers.

15   Wheeling Div.